# Cattle and Cowboys
# Letters from the 1880s

Check out Kent Brooks other titles available on Amazon.com and Lonesomeprairie.com:

*Old Boston: As Wild As They Come*

*Letters from Colorado*

*Letters from Wyoming*

# Cattle and Cowboys: Letters from the 1880s

## Compiled and Annotated

### By

### Kent Brooks

Kent Brooks

2018

All rights reserved. This book or any portion thereof may not be reproduced or used in any manner whatsoever without the express written permission of the publisher except for the use of brief quotations in a book review or scholarly journal.

First Printing: 2018

ISBN 978-1732258570

Lonesome Prairie Publications
PO Box 842
Casper, WY 82602

www.lonesomeprairie.com

Ordering Information:

Special discounts are available on quantity purchases by corporations, associations, educators, and others. For details, contact the publisher at the above listed address.

# Dedication

To those who have carried on the legend and tradition of the American Cowboy.

# Contents

Acknowledgements .................................................................. ix
Introduction ............................................................................ 1
Chapter 1: 1880 ..................................................................... 3
Chapter 2: 1881 ................................................................... 14
Chapter 3: 1882 ................................................................... 32
Chapter 4: 1883 ................................................................... 44
Chapter 5: 1884 ................................................................... 76
Photo Gallery ....................................................................... 93
Chapter 6: 1885 ................................................................... 97
Chapter 7: 1886 ................................................................. 109
Chapter 8: 1887 ................................................................. 125
Chapter 9: 1888 ................................................................. 168
Chapter 10: 1889 ............................................................... 183
Glossary ............................................................................. 216

# Acknowledgements

The idea and initial content for this work originate from the research I did for my book, *"Old Boston: As Wild As They Come."* Thanks to the historians of old who didn't have access to the resources available today. I appreciate their work more than ever. I really can't imagine putting one of these things together with a typewriter and without access to digital archives available today.

Thank you, God in heaven for the ability to work. With my brother, who had cerebral palsy, specifically in mind, not everyone is given that gift. I am humbled for the opportunity to work on compiling this small piece of history.

# Introduction

The American cowboy has long been a popular figure in fiction, motion pictures, and stories of the West. The core content in this compilation is from, cowboys, cowboy's wives, correspondents and others who wrote letters discussing feats of skill in roping, riding, and branding. They also wrote of the geography, stampedes, weather, outlaws, cattle kings, and more in these 1880s letters and reports. It may surprise some to learn of the impressive educational credentials of many cowboys who came west in the 1880s. An 1889 report in this text reports the diplomas of 63 out of 103 cowboys working for one Texas Cattle Company were from such universities as Harvard, Yale, Princeton, the University of Virginia, and other leading institutions of the land. Many of the cowboys were well prepared to record details of the cowboy experience in the American West. Emerson Hough, author of "Story of the Cowboy," also provides insight into the era of the cowboy and the cattle industry of the 1880s American West when he writes,

> *"Like everything peculiarly distinctive, the life of the cowboy through its very raciness has lent itself to literary abuse, and the cowboy has been freely pictured by indolent and unscrupulous pens as an embodiment of license and uproarious iniquity.*

*The American cowboy is the most gallant modern representative of a human industry second to very few in antiquity."*[1]

As I worked on my book *"Old Boston: As Wild As They Come"* I found myself increasingly enthralled with writers like Hough, the news of yesteryear, and even more so with the frontier newspapermen of the 1880s. The more I read these old-time newspapers…the more I read. These adventurers would report news from the west back to places from where they had come. Reports and letters were sent to and published in the local newspaper so they would not have to write multiple letters to friends and family in the same place as they reported on what they had seen out west. Some letters are from citizens or cowboys who chased adventure in the west. Other letters about the cattle industry and the cowboy of the American West were by news correspondents. The spelling errors and alternate spellings from the original letters have been retained. Examples, include terms such as "clerk" which is often spelled "clark."

The letters within these pages provide a living picture of both the cattle industry and cowboys of the 1880s. I hope you enjoy this compilation as much as I enjoyed putting it together.

---

[1] The Story of the Cowboy," by E. Hough. D. Appleton & Co., New York, 1921.

# Chapter 1: 1880

*"When a Texas cow-boy drinks too much "ole pizen" and gets on the rampage and wants to fight, about the healthiest thing a man can do is to go off to the other end of town and see if he can't organize a Sunday-school class."*

-The *Times-Democrat (*New Orleans, Orleans, Louisiana, 1880.

> **Murders by Texas Cow-Boys.**
> ST. LOUIS, January 24th. —The *Republican* has a special from Trinidad, Colorado, which says: Several hundred cowboys from Pan Handle, Texas, are said to be camped between here and Los Vegas. Fifteen of them entered Los Vegas Thursday night, killed the City Marshal and two citizens, and wounded five others.

*Oakland Tribune* (Oakland, California) 24 Jan 1880.

> **The Cow-Boys of New Mexico.**
> *Editor* GAZETTE:

**Daily Gazette (Las Vegas, New Mexico) 11 Feb 1880.** — Cowboys, taken in general, have a pretty bad reputation in the frontier towns, and from the way some of them have acted, of late around Vegas, I can't blame people much for having bad opinion of them. But a cowboy is a different being altogether when seen in the dance hall, especially when crazed by ardent spirits, from what he appears, or really is, when at home on the ranch. Besides there are generally black sheep in every flock and the majority ought not to be blamed for the doings of a few. Of course a herder has to be "heeled." As they call it out here, that is, well armed. He has to saddle his bronco in the morning and start out on his beat, a ride of not less than twenty miles, to run out stray cattle, or see that animals of his range have not passed the boundary. There are wolves, coyotes, wild cats and other animals which attack young colts and calves; these have to be killed off. Then there are horse and cattle thieves, who like to prey on isolated ranches. A cowboy would be in a pretty fix should he encounter some of these in the act of driving off stock and him not

## WELL ARMED.

Instead of recovering his own animals, the party would most certainly "put a head on him," if they would not make him help drive off his own stock under compulsion, to a safe distance. It is true, this constant presence and handling of arms leads to be aggressive, rather than on the defense, especially when coming to a town for recreation and sport. Furthermore, a cowboy, taken in general is pretty sensitive. Trying to make an honest living, at comparatively small wages, it touches his pride to even the smallest hint that there are double branded cows, or an unlawful number of mavericks on the range and should you intend to call him a thief or a liar or a son of a ____, you had better put your hands on your arms first and be prepared for war. Taken in all the cowboy reminds me of the stories I read in my schooldays of the armored knights and chevaliers of the middle ages, who upon the least pretense challenged one another to deadly battle on the field of honor. But there is one soft spot where he can't stand tickling; take him into a society of ladies — I mean ladies of the full sense of the word, and the lion of the prairie turns into a docile lamb. There the two extremities of

## COURAGE, BRAVERY AND HONOR,

and docility, gentleness and love meet. Let him unbuckle his belt and lay aside his arms and he is like a charmed bird. For hours he can talk to his girl or "old woman," if married and not a single frown can be noticed on his brow. The cares and dangers of the outdoors are forgotten; he sits by the fireside, or in the shade of the neighboring groves, making everybody burst laughing with his droll jokes, or funney yarns, if company are near, or assurances of love and devotion, it *tete-a-tete* with his dulcinea.

    These are the general characteristics of those brought up to a business from infancy; even if it be in the Lone Star State, where cattle raising is carried on more extensively than in any other State in the Union. But not every Texan is a cowboy, neither every cowboy a Texan. In the vicinity of La Cinta we have cattle herders who represent every class of society and vary business calling. The student as well as the professor; the retired merchant and his clerk, or bookkeeper; printers, mechanics and laborers have forsaken their former paths of life and taken to herding cattle; either as sole proprietors, or on shares or wages for others and of course, the cowboy here is different from

## THOSE OF ELSWHERE.

Although occupied in the same routine of business, you can easily distinguish his former training.  His behavior and every movement, when in contact with others, is more guarded and constrained.  He can break in a bronco, stay as long in the saddle, endure rain and sunshine, hardship and fatigue as well as the other; be as content in his batchelor's cabin; do his own cooking and bread baking; but don't talk to him of washing and mending; that is out of the question.  Some neighboring members of the gentle sex is called on for that, and what is best of all, be it on the ranch or in town, ardent spirits don't make our cowboys as crazy and itching for a fight as those lately seen around Las Vegas.  With this, I suppose, I will have to finish my trip to Red River; but it will not be many days before you and your readers will hear again from me on a trip down the Rio Grande.

**ROUGH DIAMOND.**

## THE COW-BOY
### On His Native Texan Plains.

**The *Times-Democrat* (New Orleans, Louisiana) 7 Sep 1880.** — Very nearly every day persons gather around the stockyards below the city and watch the large loads of cattle which are brought over the river from Morgan's depot.

Although these long horns are found roaming in a wild state on the prairie of Texas, yet the long sea voyage and the rough usage seems to gentle them, and the same can be said of the Texas cow-boy who, off his native heath, is an entirely different character.

The civilized cow-boy, seen in a rural landscape, is a very small urchin with his pants' legs rolled up, a demoralized looking suspender running in a bias course across his back, while in one hand he holds a crooked switch and drives ahead of him a couple of quiet, lazy-looking cows.

The usual fiery sunset, farmhouse, and a man leaning on a stile with a cob-pipe in his mouth are to be seen in the background. This is the gentle specimen of the cow-boy, and there is just as much difference between him and the ones who hails from Texas as there is between a black cat and a tambourine.

The Texas cow-boy is a rough, big, burly individual, as wild and just about as difficult to handle as the vicious looking mustang he rides. His costume consist of a broad sombrero, short jacket, jean pants, with the legs of them stuffed in his boots. To each boot is fastened a spur with an rowel that would discount a circular saw.

Around his waist is a Mexican sash and Colt's six-shooter which he often handles in a very careless manner. A great many people have died from the effects of it. This is the pen portrait of the genuine unsophisticated Texas cow-boy who is to be admired in somethings, and not interfered with in others.

His home is the saddle, and the prairie his bed, and after a hard day's "drive" and the round-up" made, he "hobbles" his fleet footed pony and leaves him to graze at will. After this duty is attended to, and he has cursed the cook of the herd for not having enough calf ribs roasted, he stretches himself on his blanket and snores as contentedly as a bloated millionaire, provided there is no game of poker going on. There are ties binding a cow-boy to poker which death alone can sever. The general belief that a Texas cow-boy is cut-throat of the deepest dye is false and it will not do to tell him so either.

It is true that his not as good as the young man in the Bible class, but he is far from being a villain. He is rough, but the hardships he endures makes him so, he could not be otherwise.

Often on a dark stormy night blinding flashes of lightning illuminate for an instant the inky darkness, amid the drenching rain he rides from one point of the herd to another, trying to keep the frightened cattle together, and to prevent them from stampeding if possible.

He understands what a "stampede" means, and when the wild cattle, crazed by terror at the fierceness of the storm dash out into the darkness clashing their horns and bellowing with fear, he rides abreast of the rushing herd, realizing that if his horse should stumble and fall that he would meet with a certain and horrible death, and yet a number of persons wonder why a cow-boy has so much nerves.

Young men who live in the old States, and who have read of cow-boy life imagine that it is quite romantic to gallop over the prairies wild and free, but galloping over a Texas prairie in the middle of August has about as much romance as the itch.

When a Texas cow-boy drinks too much "ole pizen" and gets on the rampage and wants to fight, about the healthiest thing a man can do is to go off to the other end of town and see if he can't organize a Sunday-school class.

If a cow-boy proclaims with a yell, "I'm a long-haired tarantula o the West," it is not safe for one to say, "I'm a fighting cayote." Quite a number of enterprising men have had a crape tied on their own door-knobs for doing so.

***Vermont Phoenix*** **(Brattleboro, Vermont) 24 Dec 1880.** — Notwithstanding that cattle, no less than sheep, are able to obtain their own subsistence all the year round, the avocation of stock-growing is attended with no little care and labor. During the summer, autumn and winter the cattle roam at will over the plains and different herds, or parts thereof, mingle, together, and perhaps wander for long distances from their home range. Very frequently single heads, separated most likely from their herd in a stampede, are found 200 miles away. To collect these stragglers, and to take a census, no less than to pick out the beeves for market the annual "round up" is held. At this period, falling in May and June, the whole country is searched, and the cattle appertaining to a district driven together in one vast herd, from whence the different ranchmen separate their own cattle, easily recognizable by the brand; and after a mutual exchange of strayed ones, each owner takes his herd back to their home range, and after branding the calves, turns them out loose, not to see them again till next year's "round up."

For each district, embracing many hundred square miles, and from 10 to 20 ranges, a captain generally one of the old settlers well acquainted with the country is chosen. Under him work the stockmen cow-boys or cow-punchers, as everybody connected with cattle-raising is called from the different ranches, numbering often 70 or more men, and 200 or more horses, for each cow-boy has three, and often as many as eight, spare mounts with him on these occasions. The whole country, so large that it will take them one or two months to work it over, is laid out in daily rides. If there is a large creek or stream in the distance the water-course is followed, the country for 20 or 30 miles on both sides being carefully searched by the mounted cow-boys, who, all working under one head, develop great aptitude for their laborious work. They are in the saddle for at least 10 hours every day, and most of the time on the "lope," or canter; often long after dark they bring in, driving before them the stock found that day, when, after watering the thirsty beasts, they are added to the main herd, which is carefully watched day and night.

If the range, as is very frequently the case, is a mountainous one there are many in Wyoming seven and eight thousand feet above the sea, in the heart of the Rocky mountains, the search for cattle is far more difficult than on level or undulating prairie land. In the former case, the rough and steep chains of mountains, full of "drars,"[2] pockets and gulches, generally densely timbered at the bottom, the search is anything but easy. A cow or small bunch of cattle, overlooked on one "round up" is, however, not necessarily lost: for generally they will turn up on that or some neighboring ranch during the next year's round up. Wyoming ranch-men have told me that often they accidentally pitch up-on cattle they misted[3] four or five years before. On such occasions the original cow will make her appearance with quite a little family of unbranded steers, yearlings and calves. Considering how broken the ground, and of what huge dimensions each range, it speaks well for the cow-boy's powers that the losses for straying amount, under proper care, to not more than 1 or 2 per cent per annum. The annual total percentage of losses incurred from stress of weather, drouths, etc., varies considerably. More than half of the owners or managers of the ranges (about 100) I visited declared that 5 per cent in average years will amply cover; others maintained 7, and a few even thought 10 per cent.

---

[2] draw
[3] missed

The round up is a busy time for man and horse on frontier ranches. It is a period affording pleasant change to the cow-boy, who the rest of the year is buried on his isolated ranch often months without seeing a white man, and years frequently pass before a petticoat makes his heart flutter. There is a wonderful amount of animated life, light-hearted merriment and vigorous and healthful rivalry about one of these round-ups. Up before sunrise, a substantial breakfast, at which often half a steer divided among the different messes is used; the rising orb sees them in the saddle, a couple of led animals on the line galloping over the plains in pursuit of those distant black specks, or ascending the dangerously steep slopes of a dismal "hog back" hill, from whence the higher ranges in the pine-clad mountains are reached. They usually do not return to camp till dusk, driving before them the cattle found by them that day, which, if it is in open country, will often be as many as 200 to the man; if broken and full of pockets and drars, or densely timbered ravines, perhaps not more than 10 or 15. Cow-boys learn to track animals as Indians do game, and I was often amused to watch from some elevated spot a "field" of cow-boys at work. Here you will see a couple dismounted and leading their ponies, following some faint tracks on the hard gravelly soil, which, until softer ground is reached, or other indisputable stock signs discovered, might prove those of elk or (unshod) Indian ponies. Generally water betrays cattle; for let them be over so far from it, or carefully screened from discovery in dense limber, they must at least once every 24 hours repair to the next creek or water-hole, when their tracks are easily discernable. Yonder we perceive three or four of the daring riders pursuing a small "bunch" stampeding down a steep slope, tails raised high, evidently frightened at the unusual sight of man, and the pursuers at full gallop tearing down the hill at more than breakneck pace, endeavoring to head them off; man and horse apparently oblivious to the steepness of the grade and the many treacherous holes and tree-stumps that dot it. They are all wonderful riders, and on these occasions they strive to outdo each other. I saw one spill on a steep hill-side, occasioned by a gopher hole, into which the horse put one of its fore-legs; and from motives of curiosity I measured the distance the rider was sent spinning, and found that between the gopher-hole and the spot where the man's shoulder touched the ground first was 37 feet less three inches. The man was only slightly stunned, and amid the laughter of his companions who never show any mercy on such occasions, picked himself up, and pulling his six-shooter forthwith shot the disabled "broncho."

# Chapter 2: 1881

*"Many cattlemen propose hereafter to discharge their cowboys[4] in October and not to employ them until May. For five months the hellions on horseback will receive $50 a month. What will they do during the other seven? They will not work except as centaurs. They will not even help to make a cow pen. The only other work that seems to commend itself to their fancy is stage driving or stage robbing. I look for a large increase in the last named industry next winter."*

-Letter from Wyoming to Ohio, 1881.

> Bent Murdock writes an entertaining letter from Trinidad, to the *Commonwealth*. He says that place is being made the headquarters for many owners of large cattle ranches.

The *Girard Press* (Girard, Kansas) 26 May 1881.[5]

---

[44] Cowboy is spelled in multiple ways in the 1880s including cowboy, cow boy and cow-boy.

[5] The Prairie Cattle Company as well as other foreign syndicates were beginning to buy up ranches in Southeast Colorado.

> **A COWBOY'S LIFE.**
>
> **Crossing the Mountains With Four Thousand Cattle.**
>
> **A Stampede in the Mountains on a Dark Night—The Nature of a Cowboy's Sleep—"Milling" Cattle.**
>
> San Francisco Chronicle.

The *Nebraska State Journal* **(Lincoln, Nebraska) 11 Mar 1881.** *Spirit of the Age* **(Woodstock, Vermont) 18 May 1881.** — "Gabriel will require a large club attachment to that horn of his, or else he will never be able to rouse the mountain cowboys," remarked Ben Heywood, Utah cattle dealer, to a *Chronicle* reporter.

"Why so" asked the reporter.

"Because," replied Heywood, "there is no circumstances under which a cowboy will not sleep if not physically molested. In the midst of a mountain storm, when the crashing thunder comes simultaneously with the glaring sheets of lighting, the cowboy sleeps peacefully, in a dry creek bed, with his head down grade, he slumbers sweetly; in view of tarantulas, rattlesnakes and centipedes for bed-fellows, he closes his eyes, and dreams of a heaven of unlimited plug tobacco and unstinted sleep. Gabriel's trumpet would indeed sound in vain when the time came to check off a drove of cowboys. Last spring I was driving four thousand head of cattle over the Rocky mountains by the south Wyoming pass, and a run — the terror of cattle-drivers — took place under circumstances which showed just how sound is the sleep of a cowboy. I had fifteen boys a "boy" with the "cow" prefix may mean a forty-year-old man with me. It takes nearly that many to start a drove of four thousand cattle, though a half-dozen boys can take care of the drove after the first week on the road. By that time the cattle know what is expected of them, and give us very little trouble.

## IN CAMP.

"Well, we were camped one night on the very summit of the mountains. The sleeping ground for the stock was in a little five-acre patch of grass; all around were sagebrush and rocks of volcanic formation. You understand that after cattle are quietly settled at night on good sleeping ground three or four, men ride in a circle around them. This is done by relays of men in 'watches,' the watch being changed at midnight I have many a time seen a cowboy at a broncho, riding round and round the drove at night fast asleep in his saddle. On the night in question I happened to be standing the first watch myself, and only had two boys with me. The night was overcast and dark, the few stars which shone between the rifts of driving clouds, just serving to outline the mass of sleeping cattle. The air seemed surcharged with electricity, and though there had been no lightning it was just such a night in which runs always occur. I have heard no end of scientific and practical explanation of stock runs or stampedes generally by men who never saw one in their lives. It is well enough to say that something frightens them, if you know nothing about it and want to explain it; but then that doesn't explain it, no way.

## CAUSE OF A RUN.

"They say that a coyote, or some other prowling beast, frightens one of a drove and that one infects the others with panic and the stampede begins. Well it ain't so. If you have a drove of a thousand or ten thousand, the panic infects every one of them at exactly the same instant. It is something harder to account for than a prowling coyote; and because a run never occurs except on such a night as I have described. Leave it to those who know all about atmospheric influences and such to tell just what it is. Anyway, I was a little uneasy that night, for one of the two boys on watch with me was only a tenderfoot; understand? A man new to the business and fresh from the east. It was nearly 12 o'clock, and I had just turned my horse's head towards camp, which was about fifty yards in the rear of tbe sleeping ground, to make up the relief watch, when the run commenced. Every one of that drove of four thousand cattle was on its feet like a flash, and exactly at the same instant. With a rush like a whirlwind that levels a forest, they were off in the darkness, the strong and heavy ones in the lead, of course. The rattling of horns and the thundering of hoofs was deafening. The effect it has on a person who experiences it for the first time was shown by the action of the tenderfoot.

## A NIGHT STAMPEDE.

"He turned his horse's tail towards the stampede, buried his spurs in his bronco's flank, and never stopped till he was out of hearing. He was crazier with fright than the wildest steer in the drove. Well, seeing $30,000 worth of stock running away from me and having had thirteen years' experience I naturally acted differently. By the specter starlight I could see the cattle outlined as a black, thundering, rushing, clattering stream, rushing wildly, and at each instant becoming wilder, over the rocks and a stretch of sagebrush. My horse was trained in the business and knew what was the trouble as well, and just as soon, too, as I did. I did not have to guide him. I followed along by the side of the stampede, and overtook the leaders. It don't do to try and turn a run too quick. I kept by the side of the leaders and quartering on them, striking their flanks and pushing gradually against them on the left, slowly turned the leaders slightly to the right. If that can be done, in a short time the line will "mill" itself. The leaders only need to be turned, the rest all blindly follow. By constantly keeping them turning to the right the leaders were swung clear around finally, and overtook the fag end of the line,

## RUNNING IN A CIRCLE.

"There they were rushing around in a circle, the centre of which soon closed up, and they were 'milling;' that is they had formed a solid wheel and kept going round and round themselves in the same pace of ground. I tell you that cowboy and myself did some tall riding around that 'mill' to keep the outside stock from tearing off at a tangent, as they will do sometimes. Little by little they slowed down, and as soon as we could make our voices heard we quieted them by singing and talking to them. There is nothing which will bring a crazy steer to his senses as quick as the sound of a human voice and if you can only sing a little you can do the work all the quicker. The clashing and crashing of horns and the pounding of hoofs grew less and less deafening; one after another would recognize our voices and slow down until, finally, almost as suddenly as it had started, the run was at an end and the cattle as quiet and well behaved as ever. In the morning the circle where the mill had been was as devoid of vegetation as a dancing hall. The sagebrush was ground to powder, and the ground looked exactly as though it had been prepared for a circus ring. Through the sage brush where the stock had run, a straight, smooth swath was cut as if by a mowing machine with a potato digging attachment. I started to say how a cowboy could sleep throughout that run, throughout the excitement, the deafening noise and the danger those cowboys in camp slept as they might in a featherbed in a Palace Hotel.

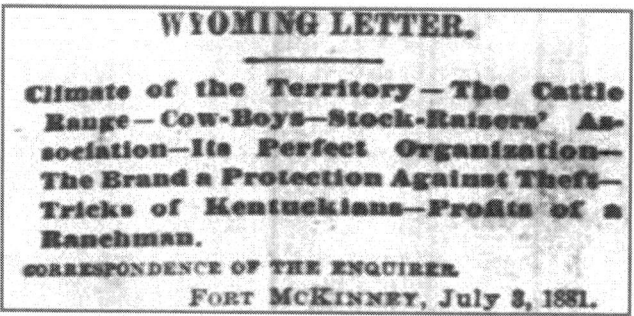

**The *Cincinnati Enquirer* (Cincinnati, Ohio) 16 Jul 1881.** — All heirs of Adam have a sentence of death read to them every day. It is this: Put beef or bread in your stomach, or you die. Hence, the importance of a new cattle range. The last and best is probably in Northern Wyoming and Southern Montana, or so much of the country as lies between the North Platte and Yellowstone Rivers, and the Big Horn Mountains and the Black Hills. The line of travel to this region is from Bock Creek Station, on the Union Pacific Railroad, by one of the now famous, or infamous, Star Routes, over the Laramie Hills to Fort Fetterman, and thence north-westwardly to Powder River. From, that to the railroad, one hundred and eighty miles, the country is a dreary wilderness, but at Powder River, you come to an excellent cattle region, far better indeed than the country further south. Why this is so I will explain. The Union Pacific Road runs westward from Omaha up the back line of the continent. The average elevation across Wyoming is about seven thousand feet. Where the stage road crosses Powder River it is only about four-thousand feet above the sea. Fort McKinney, on the Clear Fork of Powder, is a little over five thousand. From thence the country falls gradually to the Yellowstone, which is only about three thousand five hundred feet above the sea level. In round numbers, every eight hundred feet of elevation are equivalent to a degree of latitude. Upon this basis of calculation, the isotherm of the Powder River Valley would be equivalent to 52 degrees on the sea coast; that of the Yellowstone to 54 degrees; that of Cheyenne to 54 degrees.

This is merely a theoretical calculation. In point of fact, the winters here are not nearly so severe as they are in New England or New York. I refer now to the well-protected valleys of the Big Horn, Tongue River, and the Yellowstone. The high ridge from Omaha to Ogden is swept by fearful storms, and is, as everybody knows, a cold, bleak and desolate region. Fort Bridges, which is south of the railroad, but up in the mountains, is by the record the coldest military post in North America. The snow-fall of Wyoming is about equal to that of Northern Ohio. The wintering of cattle in this region without feeding must be quite a mystery to Eastern people. I believe that in Kentucky livestock has to be wintered at great expense. The explanation is this: First, the grass here is more nutritious than in the States; second, on account of the absence of moisture it cures itself and becomes hay without being cut. The cattle live, in fact, in standing fields of naturally cured hay; third, the snow is drier and far lighter than the snow on lower levels. It soon blows off the hillsides, and cattle soon learn to seek it where they can most easily get it. They soon begin to dig for it like bison, antelope or elk. Last winter was the most severe ever known in this region, yet the loss even of the Texas cattle was only 10 percent; of Montana, or acclimated, cattle, only 5 percent, were lost. One man put in a drove of Kentucky stock and lost nearly all of them. But he took a notoriously bad range and made the great mistake of herding his cattle in winter. It is found better to let them run without any attempt at herding. Many cattlemen propose hereafter to discharge their cow boys in October and not to employ them until May. For five months the hellions on horseback will receive $50 a month. What will they do during the other seven? They will not work except as centaurs. They will not even help to make a cowpen. The only other work that seems to commend itself to their fancy is stage driving or stage robbing. I look for a large increase in the last named industry next winter.

It may seem inexplicable to the uninitiated that a man is in no more danger of losing his cows wandering over these boundless prairies than if they are in a Scioto or Miami pasture. This comes from the perfect organization of the Stock Raisers Association. This company has its inspectors at every point from which cattle are driven or shipped to the East. They have, of course, the brands of all the members. If one member who is shipping cattle gets some of another member's beeves in his brand, as often happens, the fact is reported by the inspectors, who note every brand on every beef that passes every station. The shipper is compelled to settle with all the members whose stray cattle may have got into his lot. So well do the inspectors do their work that all attempts at theft are at once discovered, and the thief is prosecuted at the expense of the Association. All depredations on the ranges are reported to the officers of the company, who at once send detectives to work the case. The stealing of a steer is far more serious on the plains than killing a man. A ludicrous instance of the zeal of the cattlemen in these prosecutions came to my notice a short time since. A rich man from Chicago, who is in the cattle business rode up to a granger's ranch and asked for dinner. A meal was soon cooked for him, at which he had fresh beef. So far, so good. But after his repast the gentlemen from the great Lake City looked around to find the hide of the beef of which he had partaken. He could not find it. The next night he sent up a lot of corrals to drag the creek to find the beef, they could not find it. Then, the gentleman offered a reward of $1,000 for the discovery of the missing hide. This may seem like midsummer madness to people in your longitude, but the fact is that the gentleman granger was suspected of having very promiscuous ideas in regard to the rights, of persons and the rights of things. Hence this eagerness of the stockmen to introduce him to John Doe and Richard Roe. In the Isle of Wight, it was a felony to steal a chicken and only a misdemeanor to steal a cow because a chicken could be hidden there and a cow could not; but here a cow is as sacred a divinity as she was in ancient Egypt.

Great efforts are being made to improve the stock hereabouts. Some very fine Durhams have been brought from Kentucky. All the larger owners are raising high grade cattle. By the way, one of our patriarchs who has been over to the Blue Grass Regions to buy a bull thinks he has discovered that even the high-toned Kentuckians have tricks in trade quite surprising. He says that whenever one Blue Grass Lord buys at the fancy stock sales a $15,000 cow from a neighbor that neighbor always buys two calves from the party of the first part at exactly the same price, and no money passes. Great Scott! Can this be true? If so, then Touchstone's denunciation of those who make their living by the copulation of cattle is well founded. One of our cattle kings has announced his intention of hereafter raising nothing but thoroughbreds. The success of this man in the business deserves a passing notice, ten years ago he was selling wood to a Government post and driving one of his own teams. Then he borrowed money at 2 1/2 percent, a month and went into the cattle business. Within the last few weeks he has sold one brand of cattle for $100,000, another for

$130,000. Besides this he has built a $20,000 house, and fenced a pasture lot forty miles square. He is selling out his common stock to raise lovely white-nosed short horns. By the way, this Western philosopher has not confined his wish to improve aboriginal stock to cattle. He is also raising a family of human half-breeds. Some time ago he went to his copper-colored companion and said to her, "You must either marry me and live in a house, or I will give you $20,000 to go back to your tribe." The fair barbarian chose the former alternative. So Miss White Bear Paw became Mrs. Jones, and the $20,000 was spent on a house.

I have never seen as fine a class of settlers in any new Territory as we have here in Wyoming. We have many people of education and refinement. There are hereabout a number of business men from Chicago, tempted out by profits that seem almost incredible. I will give you a statement of the increase on 1,000 given me by the nearest ranchman, which he assures me is based on actual experience:

| | |
|---|---|
| First year's increase, 1,000 cows—90 per cent.—one-half males | 450 |
| Second year—one-half males | 450 |
| Third year, 1,450 cows—90 per cent. produce—one-half males | 652 |
| Fourth year, 1,900 cows—one-half males | 855 |
| Fifth year, 2,552 cows—one-half males | 1,148 |
| Total males | 3,555 |
| First year's increase, 1,000 cows—90 per cent.—one-half females | 450 |
| Second year—one-half females | 450 |
| Third year, 1,450 cows—90 per cent. produce—one-half females | 652 |
| Fourth year, 1,900 cows—one-half females | 855 |
| Fifth year, 2,552 cows—one-half females | 1,148 |
| Total females | 3,555 |
| Total increase | 7,110 |
| Original cows | 1,000 |
| Total | 8,110 |

There are now between Powder River and Tongue River 90,800 cattle, and several large herds are coming in. Five years ago the Indian held this country. A son of Senator Beck, of Kentucky, has a flock of sheep on Goose Creek which wintered well and is doing well. This is the only experiment that has been made in the sheep line in this vicinity. Excellent crops of small grain and vegetables can be raised here by irrigation. There are no mines in this part of the Territory, yet it is absolutely certain that there is gold in the Big Horn range of mountains. Gold has been found in many of the streams running from the range, but not in paying quantities. It might pay anyone who has money enough to gamble on the chances to grub, stake some prospectors and make the experiment. The indications are that gold could be found in certain places on the Crow Reservation, but it would be by no means healthy to go there at present.

**THOMAS M. ANDERSON.**

# COWBOYS.

## The Wild Life of the Cattle-Herders on the Southern Border.

### One Minister Compelled to Take a Big Drink And Another to Dance Before His Congregation.

### A Leaf From the History of the Notorious Jack Slade — Cattle-Stealing On the Plains.

**Omaha Daily Bee (Omaha, Nebraska) 3 Aug 1881.** — Tucson, Ariz., Cor. Chicago Tribune. I met a "rara avis" on the train today, "between Tucson and Benson, in the person of a noted cow-boy named Jerry Benton. He had killed a man two or three weeks ago, and was on his way to the scene of the murder for trial. "The law gets the best of us follows," said he to me as he laid a huge six-shooter on the seat in front and took a seat by my side. "I have a chance for my life if only one man is against me, but a dozen against one give's a fellow no show. But in my bondsmen shan't suffer, and I'll stand my trial like a man." He was a burly follow, with the white slouch hat, colored shirt, scarred face, and desperado look so characteristic of the border-ruffian, and with a form which whisky and a wild life seemed powerless to deform. "Jerry is a good fellow," said his companion to me as Jerry placed his revolver in his belt and walked to the other end of the car, "but a regular devil when angry or under the influence of liquor." He has killed so many men that he now takes no chances, and thinks that almost every man he meets is after his life. That huge revolver he carries is dangerous weapon, and Jerry generally knows how to 'get the drop on his victim; but the last young man he killed was very popular with his friends, and some strange swearing may be expected at the trial. Arizona is a frontier country, and a man must not be squeamish about shooting if he himself expect to survive; still, there is a great deal of honor among cowboys, and Jerry is not the least honorable of them all.

## COWBOY CHARACTERISTICS.

Jerry Benton is only the type of a class of men who are scattered through Arizona, New Mexico, Colorado, and Texas, and who are more dangerous to society than all the other criminal classes combined. The untamed cowboy generally sports a large six-shooter, a belt, a knife, repeating rifle, and and huge pair of spurs; while the mustang which he rides is supplied with a Spanish saddle, and held in and guided by a huge Spanish bit. Herding cattle being his vocation, nothing delights him more than a wild chase after an untamed steer; and, being a splendid rider, neither an Apache nor a soldier can get the best of him on the plains. Sometimes he is an American, sometimes a Mexican, a half-breed, or Indian; but, no matter what his nationality may be is as uncivilized as a grizzly bear and reckless as a savage.

He would be as much out of place in a Chicago parlor as a wolf in a sheepfold or an alligator in a bird-cage; but, properly mounted, his saddle, ornamented, and, his animal trained; to carry out his slightest wish, he does not serve as a bad subject for an artist, and his physique and horsemanship are universally praised. Quick, wiry, and intrepid, often generous and humane, he is ever sui generis, and many are the stories told of his bloodthirsty career. Originally he belonged to Texas and was generally known as the Texas ranger; but, with the increase in stock-raising farther west, he has finally come upon the railroad, and is now found on every range from Tucson to Santa Fe. He it is who has made life on the border unsafe for immigrants, who does the shooting in most of our frontier towns, and who is fast becoming a terror to the citizens of the section which he chooses to visit. Like "the bad man from Bodie," fear to him is an unknown quantity, and the greater the danger the more desperate he seems to become.

## PRACTICAL JOKES.

Some time ago a crowd of cowboys went to a certain restaurant in a small town north, and amused themselves by shooting at the plates in front of the boarders. The guests suddenly concluded that they were no longer hungry, a general stampede was made, and the cowboys enjoyed the fun immensely,

"A cowboy came into my place once near Tombstone," said Jerry Benton to me as we journeyed across Arizona, "and began firing at my chandelier. I began firing, too; and soon that cowboy dropped into his tracks."

In another village, not long since, I read that, after a certain congregation had assembled in the evening, a number of cowboys entered the church, and one of them exclaimed: "See how neatly I can shoot the eye out of that fool of a preacher!" The preacher stepped down and out, and the congregation quickly dispersed.

"Curley Bill," who killed Marshal White at Tombstone last year with his gang entered the church at Charleston, and, ordering the minister out of the pulpit, compelled him to dance in the most approved style before his congregation. The gang guarded the doors, and allowed no one to escape until the performance was over. The minister is now more opposed to dancing than before.

Another reverend gentleman not long since met two cowboys, and, on being invited to drink, politely declined. "You drink with us or die right here," said one of the desperados pointing a revolver at the minister's head. And immediately he took the biggest drink of whisky he had ever taken in his life; and even Neal Dow, John B. Gough, or Gov. St John would not otherwise have acted.

"Johnny Behind the Deuce," "Buckskin Sam," "Dare-Devil Tom, and "Lightning Bill" are celebrated for their wild exploits, and sorry will be their fate if once they come within the power of the law. A few day ago "Buckskin Sam," says a San Francisco correspondent, bought a new gun in a store on the border, and celebrated his purchase by riding through the streets and firing it off. A great excitement was the consequence, and armed men on foot and horses at once gathered and gave chase. Sam, however, eluded them, and, after having no small amount of fun, came in and gave himself up, and the next day paid a handsome fine into the city treasury,

## A SPECIMEN DESPERADO.

It is related of the notorious Jack Slade who at one time haunted the region of the north, and that whom no more desperate cowboy has since appeared, that, on one occasion finding an old enemy tied to a post by his (Jack's) friends. In such a position as to render him helpless, he shot him, twenty-three times, taking care not to kill him, cursing all the time in the most fearful manner, and taking a drink between every two shots. While firing the first twenty-two shots he would tell his victim just where he was going to hit him, and then send a ball to the spot indicated. Seven of Slade's companions witnessed the proceedings, and thought it was capital fun. Unable to provoke a sign of fear from the helpless enemy, he thrust his pistol into his month, and at the twenty-third shot blew his enemy's head to pieces. Slade then cut off the ears, which he afterwards was accustomed to exhibit in Saloons, and, demanding drinks on the bloody pledges, he was seldom refused.

On the frontier these cowboys are feared more than the Apaches. They shoot at a man's hat to see the man jump, and then shoot the man if he demur. They come in crowds to the smaller towns, brandish their weapons in view of the citizens whom they meet, and then help themselves to any goods or whisky which they may find. They drive cattle across the Mexican border where they sell them to their "Greaser" friends, and then steal the same cattle and drive them north, where they sell them again. Sometimes one is found who is humane, possibly generous to a fault; but a wild life on the plains is not generally adapted to bring out the better qualities of a man's life, and the majority of the cowboys in the south are a bloodthirsty and daring set.

## RELIEF MEASURES PROPOSED.

If the cattle stealing be not stopped, serious complications are likely at any time to arise between the governments of the United States and Mexico. Not long since, Gen. Fremont recommended that a force of militia be put into the field, and the governments of Sonora and Chihuahua were requested to act with the American authorities in exterminating the outlaws. "No man is safe in the interior without a revolver," said a Tuscon citizen to me "either hanging from a belt, or conveniently placed in an inside pocket." Until this dangerous class of men disappear, frontier life in New Mexico and Arizona will not possess many harms for the immigrant, and the agricultural and mining development of both territories will be seriously retarded.

**A. R. W.**

# Chapter 3: 1882

*"One of the most exciting events on the ranch is the "round up" which occurs in June and July and September and October each year. During the year the herds intermingle and stray from ranch to ranch and at certain seasons they must be collected and separated. They are distinguished by brands which are conclusive and universally accepted evidence of ownership."*

-Letter from Wyoming to Pennsylvania, 1882.

**Cowboys Terrorize a Town.**

OMAHA, January 19th.—A party of cowboys from the up country rode into Lone Pine, Tuesday night, and took possession of the town. They shot out the lamps in the saloons, riddled the windows, fixtures and walls and terrorized the inhabitants by firing fully a thousand shots during the night. Finally, a part of the gang boarded a departing train, shooting from the rear platform. The inhabitants are too glad to have escaped personal injury to think of bringing the ruffians to justice.

*Oakland Tribune* (Oakland, California) 19 Jan 1882.

—Dick Rodgers, a Colorado cowboy, rode into Fort Garland and ordered a soldier to light a cigar for him. The response was a bullet through his heart.. Jim Catson, a stage robber, who accompanied Rodgers, tried to retreat, but was given a desperate wound.

*Reno Gazette-Journal* (Reno, Washoe, Nevada) 13 May 1882.

## Our Colorado Letter.
Special Correspondence.
COLORADO SPRINGS, Aug. 12, 1882.

The *Carbon Advocate* (Lehighton, Pennsylvania) 19 Aug 1882. — It is said that there is no prettier place in Colorado than this, and no doubt it is true. Unlike Pueblo, both the town and its surrounding present features of attractiveness and the air is exceedingly bracing and delightful. The town is situated upon a slightly elevated plateau with plenty of room to spread itself out; the streets are regularly laid out with an abundance of growing shade trees, and there is everywhere a cozy appearance and an atmosphere of cleanliness and thrift. Without having reference to the last census the population would be estimated at about 6,000, and probably that is nearly correct. In this now rich and fertile valley skirting along the base of the mountains to Denver, and which was formerly but the continuation of the same sandy plain we have just left behind, we see the striking results produced by irrigation and labor. And among the curiously interesting features of a view of this valley are the unmistakable evidences that it was once a mountain plateau of several hundred feet higher elevation. The Denver & Rio Grande narrow gauge road winds a crooked and picturesque path along the base of the mountains making the 120 miles from Pueblo to Denver in about four hours, this point being a sort of half-way stopping place between the two cities or only forty-five miles from the latter.

The title of "Saratoga of the West" is claimed for Colorado Springs and Manitou, which, though three miles apart are considered in the same category. The mineral springs are the attraction at Manitou the name given to a few hotels and cottages located around the springs and at the foot of Pike's Peak. Many spend several weeks here alternately between the two especially the fashionably inclined, as here is more of the ways and manners of a fashionable resort than anywhere else in Colorado. At the Manitou Hotel the ladies "dress" for dinner as elaborately as at Cape May or Long Branch. The Spring waters are strongly charged with carbonic acid and contain carbonates of soda, lime, and magnesia in various proportions. Broad claims are made for the medicinal properties of these waters, the opinions of professors of chemistry being quoted to the effect that they excel the "Ems" and the "Spa," two of the most famous groups in Europe. The elevation of this little city is higher than that of Denver, or a little over

6,700 feet. There are splendid drives in all direction, and within a radius of seven or eight miles are numerous attractions and points of special interest, including Garden of Gods, Glen Eyrie, Ute Pass, and Mountain Park. The formations from which the latter takes its name are among the greatest curiosities to be seen in Colorado. Pen cannot well describe them. They consist of a series of curiously shaped, natural monuments which have been formed from sandstone rock solely by the notion of the weather a thin strap of iron on the top having protected these particular pieces and preserved them. No accurate estimate can be made of the hundreds of years this work of the elements has been in progress. There are perhaps a hundred of the peculiar formations of different sizes and shapes, some of which are really fantastic. The Garden of the Gods is also a remarkable freak of nature, partaking somewhat more of the grand and imposing. It is a secluded spot, hemmed in by great rocks stood up on edge and on end. They are some of the more marked of the numerous evidences on every hand here of a grand upheaval some time in the past. Imagine tremendous flat rocks large enough to cover a quarter of an acre of ground, standing up on edge, 330 feet high, and you will have some idea of what forms the chief wonder of this garden.

Upon the plains all about here may be seen vast herds of cattle and sheep. Next to mining, stock-raising is the largest interest in Colorado. All other branches of agricultural pursuits are conducted under difficulties and but a comparatively small proportion of the vast area of the State is suited to cultivation. No fruits of any kind are raised, though wheat is a successful crop, and I am told that something over 200,000 bushels in excess of the amount required for home consumption have been raised this year. But the country is better suited to grazing, and that avocation is found to be easier and more profitable. It is claimed that any man possessing knowledge of the business can reasonably calculate upon doubling once in four years whatever amount of capital he puts into it. Yet, of course, there are some risks as in every business and men without capital or acquaintances with the peculiarities of the country are not advised to go into it. Nearly all the stock-men who embarked a few years ago, however, are now immensely wealthy. The climate is so mild, especially in the southern part of the State and in New Mexico, that stock run out all winter without feeding and come out pretty well in the spring. It is astonishing how fat they will become roaming over these broad plains which look so barren, The short grass appears to be thin and worthless, but as a matter of fact, appearances are very deceiving in this case. This "buffalo grass" is about four times as nutritious, as the best Timothy. There are some very large cattle owners in Colorado. The late John Iliff who died five years ago, had at the time of his death nearly 100,000 head, on his range extending along the Platte river to Julesburg on the Union Pacific road. Mr. Farmer of Denver has about 35,000 on his range a few miles from that city. And there are others who have from 10,000 to 60,000 head. This is also a fine sheep country, the dry climate rendering them free from such ills as scab, foot rot, etc. Cattle and sheepmen do not get along well together, however, as cattle will not graze where sheep are, and sheep will soon destroy a grazing ground. On this account there has been a great deal of trouble between them in the past, whole herds of sheep having been poisoned in a night, resulting in quarrels by which several lives have been lost. Small sheep herds are to be seen in many, portions of the State, but the ranges of the big herds commence about Colorado Springs, thence south into New Mexico. Colorado ships a vast amount of wool to the East every year. There are a great many Mexicans in Southern Colorado engaged in sheep raising, some of whom have from 2,000 to 5,000 head. The Mexican sheep shear about four pounds of wool per annum.

The time when stock-raisers catch it is on the occasion of such a hard winter as they had here two years ago. At that time hay sold at $300 per ton in the San Juan country, though this is nothing compared to the earlier days before irrigation when hay sold at twenty-five cents per pound, and green grass was as scarce as hen's teeth. It is related that in the summer of 1860 an old Frenchman made a snug little raise at packing grass up from what is called the Flowery District on an old horse. This grew in bunches about a rod apart, was about the thickness of a tiding whip, and from six to eight feet long. Having no scales, the old man used to count his hay out, giving from three to five stalks for a pound. When this kind of hay was criticized by his customers, the good old man who did his mowing with a hatchet, was wont to say, "Ah, sare, I agree wis you. Zee hay is a leetle course, but he is very succulent. Besides, I give zee good weight I nevaire cut one hay in two – nevaire, sare; nevaire."

**DOM PEDRO.**

**LETTER FROM COLORADO.**
Special Correspondence.]
CAÑON CITY, COL., Oct. 28, 1882.

***Wyoming Democrat*** **(Tunkhannock, Pennsylvania) 17 Nov 1882.**
— The country about Canon City, as indicated in my last letter, is largely devoted to grazing. In fact, stock raising, or "herding," is the great industry for this whole region from Texas to a point considerably north of the Union Pacific Railway excepting the comparatively narrow limits within which mining interests are confined. In New Mexico, in Southern Colorado, on the Arkansas and its tributaries the Fountain, the St. Charles, the Muddy, the Cucharas, the Huerfano, and others in the great parks over across the range, and over the plains in Colorado, Nebraska and Wyoming, the herds roam and the rancheros ride. The progress of settlement and the advance of civilization has encroached somewhat upon what was formerly the domain of the ranchman especially in Nebraska and Northern Colorado; but, in general terms, largely covers the territory outlined above. Between Denver and Julesburg, on the Union Pacific Railroad, lays the immense range of the late John Cliff, one side of which was fifty miles

in length, and which was in all respects the most extensive ranch in Colorado. He is said to have begun on a capital of $100, and when he died four years ago his estate was valued at $1,500,000. Probably, all things considered, Southern Colorado possesses greater advantages for herding than can be combined in any part of the region devoted to that industry. It is traversed by railroads and is accessible from all sides, while the climate is most salubrious and so mild in winter that stock roam and graze without shelter or feeding. Barren as these sandy plains appear, the coarse, dry-looking tufts of "buffalo grass" furnish nutriment upon which cattle thrive and fatten beyond belief. To some there is a sentimental drawback in the absence of the grand, ever present spectacle and genuine companionship of the "everlasting hills," but that soon becomes to be a small matter when the other advantages of this locality are considered. No doubt in other regions land can be had more cheaply, but there are sure to be counterbalancing disadvantages. Above a certain latitude, notably in Wyoming, great losses have occurred from severe winters, and not very far to the north the "Lo family" come in to disturb and molest. Speaking of hard winters, they had one here in Colorado two years ago which, according to all accounts, takes the cake, and was the cause of heavy losses to cattle men. In some parts of the State hay sold at $300 per ton. But seasons like that are few and far between. Of the profits of ranching I shall not undertake, for lack of space, to give any complete estimates, though several that are full and reliable have been furnished me. After allowing for all contingencies it may be safely put down as more certain in its results than mining, and more remunerative for the capital and labor invested than the best mercantile business I know of in the East. To engage in it successfully requires capital, a knowledge of the business, sound judgment, and a willingness to endure the privations and loneliness of the life it entails. Any man with these prerequisites can certainly double an investment of $10,000 or $20,000 in five years, with a strong probability of doing much better even than that. I am told of a case where some gentlemen about ten years ago made up the sum of $7,000 for the purchase of cattle and put the herd in the hands of a practical man. It was, of course, when cattle were considerably cheaper than they are now, and they did not buy much land but sent their herd to range at a distance; but these men have since withdrawn their original investment and are offered $125,000 for what they now hold, after having allowed the manager one-quarter for his services. This may hardly be considered an average example, but it is one case of many, and a fair illustration of the possibilities of the business. Where else in the world and in what other known way can a man sit and see his possessions increase before his eyes with so little exertion on his part.

Only those who have seen the life of a ranchman as it is can have a correct idea of the fascination it possesses. To ride over the range and see the vast herds of cattle the splendid bulls, the plump steers, the red, and white, and roan, and mottled cows grazing contentedly from dawn until near noon when they all take their accustomed trail and seek the water with unerring certainty, is a study of more interest than might be imagined.  One may meet engaged in this occupation, or sitting in the door-ways of hotels here in the evenings, surrounded by "honest miners" in overalls gentleman accustomed to the resources and habits of the most refined civilization.  No one's felt hats have broader brims, no one's flannel shirts are rustier, and no one's boots more thoroughly covered with adobe dust; and everyone will tell you he is as happy as a king.  It may occur to more than one young man, conscious of the drawbacks of a business life in our cities, with its fierce competition and unavoidable risks, that life on the plains might give him ample occupation, comfortable gains and a sound mind and body.  And another class to whom this life might appeal with great force, comprises those unfortunates who seek Aiken and Florida every winter and "come home with the strawberries" in the spring.

    One of the most exciting events on the ranch is the "round up" which occurs in June and July and September and October each year.  During the year the herds intermingle and stray from ranch to ranch and at certain seasons they must be collected and separated.  They are distinguished by brands which are conclusive and universally accepted evidence of ownership.  For each district a master or director of the "round up" is chosen whose orders are implicitly obeyed by the force of from 20 to 50 men furnished by the ranch owners according to their holdings.  They have two or three horses apiece, with cooks, etc., and starting from a given point take a regular course, camping out at night.  They thus sweep the range with the skill coming from long practice and gather the cattle together, when they are separated by the brands. To witness this process and the exploits of the skillful drivers, whose trained horses "turn on a five cent piece," is a most interesting sight. There are some sheep about here, but sheep herding has been mostly driven further south by the antagonisms between sheep and cattle men, of which I may give you some fact hereafter.

**DOM PEDRO.**

## A BIG STORY.

The *Daily Republican* **(Monongahela, Pennsylvania) 29 Aug 1882.** — Mr. Robert McKean of Lock No. 4. who has gone to the Black Hills, writes us a very interesting letter from Wyoming, which will be read with great pleasure, on account of the well-known care with which he observes.

'Si Carmack hands us the following item clipped from a Rocky Mountain paper, and says that he knows it is true, for he was on the train himself: A Wyoming man saw a Texas steer standing on the railroad track, and knowing that the express train was due, tried to induce the beast to move. Several pieces of board thrown at the ferocious monster failed to move it, until at last, as the train rushed down the track at lightning speed, he seized the steer by the tail and twisted it like a wet towel. At this moment the train struck them both and the result was stupendous. The steer was found two days afterward browsing peacefully in a corn-field, with two driving wheels hung on its horns. No trace of either the man or the engine has been heard of since.

> One of the secretaries got a letter the other day, thought to be from a cow-boy in Texas, telling him if the money on a policy of certain number was not paid pretty soon that he and every member of his company would be shot on sight. The lives of five incorporators have had a price set upon them. By the way, it would take a pretty good squad of cow boys to whip out the associated forces at this place. They are as numerous as dangerous.

The *Pulaski Citizen* (Pulaski, Giles, Tennessee) 7 Dec 1882.

# Chapter 4: 1883

*"The writers for the press and illustrated magazines are in a great measure responsible for calling public attention to the Western plains and the Rocky Mountain valleys as desirable localities for cattle breeding. The majority of those writers know absolutely nothing about the breeding and successful handling of cattle. They could not distinguish a Durham steer from a scalawag Texan."*

-The New York Sun, 1883

> **TEXAN DARE-DEVILS.**
>
> **The Genuine "Cow-Boy" Comparatively Free from Vice,**
>
> **But the "Rustler" is a Terror, and Capable of Committing Almost Any Crime.**
>
> "Vet Temple" in Cincinnati Enquirer.

The *Butte Weekly Miner* **(Butte, Montana) 20 Jun 1883.** — The genuine Texas cow-boy is a character, and, after some acquaintance with him, I can say that he is one that is very little understood by the outside world. He is rough, uncouth, hardy, generous, and crave. He must stand the hardships that he takes upon himself, and be a splendid specimen of physical manhood. He is generally from twenty to thirty years of age. There are no old men in their ranks. They can beat the Mexican vaqueros (equestrians) at their own peculiar feats of horsemanship, such as picking pieces of money from the ground with their horses at a dead run. A great sport with them is called the chicken game. They bury a fowl in light earth so that nothing but the head is shown. They then ride their horses in a circle upon a keen gallop, and snatch tor the head. The man who first secures the chicken wins the prize, which is usually a small sum of money. It is a Mexican custom, but the Texan can beat him at it every time. The genuine cow-boy is comparatively free from vice in the true meaning of the term. His home is in the saddle, and he sits a horse as though he were a part of it. He frequently rides seventy miles a day, and a majority of his nights are spent in the open air. Indeed, for most of the year he never sees a house, and has no chance, if he should have the inclination, to drink liquor.

Every cow-boy labors to be a dead shot. When he gets to town, either by accident or after the year's hurry is over, he is apt to be free with his pistol if he gets drunk and finds a quarrel, as he often does. Of the petty crimes he knows nothing. He never steals unless he is dead-broke, and then he captures a horse. He never lies or cheats. The pilgrim or the tenderfoot, as they call an eastern man, is always welcome to a share of their rude fare. You can offer them no greater insult than to offer pay for it. They have an idea of social distinctions, and "Jack always rates, himself as good as his master." He very frequently has an interest in the herd he is tending, and often graduates from a cow-boy to a proprietor of a ranch. It is a joke that many of the rich men here began with only two steers and a branding-iron. Their highest idea of property being stock, they look upon homicide as an insignificant crime compared with horse-stealing. Their isolation from society, their rude life and ruder sports, make them a rough but not a dangerous set, in the sense in which they are rated at the east. Such a life naturally breeds some bad men, but it is a fact that in the bands of "rustlers" and cut-throats along the border there are more hard characters from the northern states than from the Texas cow-boys.

The "rustler" is a new creation of frontier life. He may be a horse thief, a murderer, a "busted" freighter, a discharged soldier, or a Texas cow-boy who has stolen a horse and ran away from the ranch where he was employed. By long odds the largest per cent, of them are hard characters from the east, many of whom have had liberal educations. They come out here on the border and join other lawless characters either for gain, adventure, or both. Russian Bill and Handy King, from New York, recently lynched near the Texas line, are good types of this class. Russian Bill spoke four or five languages fluently, and had no superior as a mining engineer. These rustlers were a year ago a terror to the whole frontier. They were smugglers, cattle-thieves, robbers, or were capable of committing almost any other crime. The curious feature of their existence is that they operated for and sold their plunder to people who were considered respectable. They terrorized the whole border, until at last decent people were obliged to unite for their suppression. Many good citizens were put in peril in the effort to break up these lawless gangs. But they have been broken by harsh measures, and the border is now comparatively free of them. It is but fair to say that they were not a product of the rude civilization of Texas

## THE CATTLE BUSINESS.
### Concentration of Capital—Ranches of 500,000 Acres.

*Chicago Tribune* (Chicago, Illinois) 25 Jul 1883. — [Cheyenne Letter in Philadelphia *Press*.] — One thing is plain: the method of forming combinations and consolidating separate interests into a few hands which has characterized railroad and manufacturing interests East has taken almost entire possession of the stock business here. Since the beginning of the season the number of ranches sold out to a few powerful buyers is estimated at Over 200. Such great corporations as the Swan Bros., Gilchrist & Windsor, Rand & Co., and the Powder River Cattle Company have absorbed a great many ranches, some of which have been regarded as very large and prosperous. Foreign capital is largely concerned in these transfers. For instance it is well-known that Mr. Swan of the company first named above, has been but a temporary manager for a syndicate possessing immense capital, resident in Edinburg which has purchased all the Swan Bros. cattle for $2,500,000. The Powder River Company as well with a capital of £300,000 has a directory composed of the Duke of Manchester, Lord Neville, Messers. Sartoris and Kemp and other Englishmen of wealth. These people have paid 50 per cent more for their cattle than they would have been asked a twelvemonth since.

Then I saw but the other day a gentleman returning through here from Laramie who. I was informed, represented a large accretion or capital in the East. He had been to the Cheyenne and Arapahoe Agency. Indian Territory, and purchased from the Cheyenne and Arapahoe Indians $500,000 acres of grass land from each with the privilege of fencing. He was in some doubt about interference from the Government as the leases have yet to be approved by the Secretary of the Interior before they can be acted upon, but said if all went smoothly the ranch buildings would be put up at once. He claimed that the land at present was valueless to the Indians and his purchase would give almost every Indian inhabitant of the reservation an annual income of $10 apiece.

Even while I am writing am informed authoritatively by a friend of the Swan Brothers room I mentioned just now as having sold out to the wealthy company from Edinburg and Dundee. Scotland, that they, the brothers, have formed the Swan Land & Cattle Company, in which Chicago and Milwaukee capital is largely interested. Then there are the Standard Stock Company, in North Cheyenne with a capital of least $550,000: Pratt & Farris on the North Platte. worth about the same or more; the company just formed at the head of Running Water in Wyoming with an immense capital and finally the American Land & Cattle Syndicate, organized a couple of months ago at Kansas City.

This latter is now fast completing the details of its organization some of which will make trouble in the cattle business, or I am mistaken. It is a concentration of capital of great strength and aims to the exclusive control of large domains in the southwestern territories. It will have branch offices in New York and London as well as Texas. Its membership includes some of the wealthiest business men, land and cattle owners in Kansas City. Both the United States Senators from Kansas and the Governor of the State are members.

In the far Southwest it is just the same. The largest transactions in cattle ever made in the country barring one have been made in Fort Worth and Gainsville, Texas aggregating over $2,300,000. But I am not attempting to print a catalog, only to show a tendency. And it is the most natural one in the world. "What's the use of our small ranches?" asked of me a drover with the air of a questioner who can answer his conundrums best himself. "It costs but little more to protect a large lot of cattle than it does a small one; 500 head will scatter in grazing as far as 10,000. You've got to have about as many horses and saddles and boys for the round-up and branding. There's no proportion at all in the profits."

> **Cattle Growing.**
>
> The immensity of the cattle raising business of the northwest is fairly indicated by the following extract from a Johnson county (Wyoming) letter to the Cheyenne Sun. Johnson county lies in the Powder river valley, a few miles west of the Hills, and five years ago did not contain a head of stock:

The *Daily Deadwood Pioneer-Times* (Deadwood, South Dakota) 27 Jul 1883. — The immensity of the cattle raising business of the northwest is fairly indicated by the following extract from Johnson county (Wyoming) letter the Cheyenne Sun. Johnson county lies in the Powder river valley, a few miles west of the Hills, and five years ago did not contain a head of stock. In a communication to the Sun dated the 10th inst, I stated that the total valuation of property in Johnson county for 1883, would be $3,000,000, which amount it might safely be estimated that nine-tenths was represented in the cattle interest.

Since that time I have made a more careful examination of the assessment books and find that the number of cattle of all descriptions will foot up 140,446. The assessed number is estimated to be 30 percent less than the actual number given on the books of the various owners. Taking 200,000 to be the estimated number in Johnson county, at an average price of $14 a head, it would make the total valuation $2,800,000.

The following is the price list adopted the assessors in making out the assessment: Texas yearlings, $9, two's. $11.50, cows, $14, beeves. $19; native yearlings, $11, two's, $15, cows, $20 beeves, cow ponies, $30; work animals, real value: native broodmares; $50 sheep, $2; hogs, real value.

> **THE TRUTH CONCERNING THE CATTLE RANGES ON THE WESTERN PLAINS.**
>
> Dispelling the Glamour of Cattle Raising—The Books versus the Herds—How Capitalists are Taken In—How the Government is Robbed of its Best Land.
>
> MEDICINE BOW, July 12.—

**The *Sun* (New York, New York) 22 Jul 1883.**[6] — The high price of beef has greatly stimulated the business of cattle breeding. English and Eastern capital eagerly seeks investment in western cattle ranches. It has been estimated that about $30,000,000 of English and Eastern money has been invested in the region extending from the Rio Grande River to the northern boundary line during the past three years. This is probably an over estimate. The brands that are supposed to represent ownership of horned stock are bought without a thorough examination of the herds that sanguine Investors suppose are represented by the piles of branding irons lying around corrals or

---

[6] This story caused numerous reactions as you will see in the letters that follow. It is not a letter but provides context for the letters that follow.

sketched in books of record in county offices. At present the excitement about cattle approaches the intensity of a mining craze. The writers for the press and illustrated magazines are in a great measure responsible for calling public attention to the Western plains and the Rocky Mountain valleys as desirable localities for cattle breeding. The majority of those writers know absolutely nothing about the breeding and successful handling of cattle. They could not distinguish a Durham steer from a scalawag Texan. Their knowledge is obtained from the fraudulently kept stock books and lying statements made by ranchmen who are anxious to unload on English and Eastern investors The impression conveyed by these writers is that the Western plains and mountain valleys team with herds of cattle fueling on the nutritious grasses and that certain wealth awaits all men who will pay attention to their herds. Descriptions of life on the plains and in the mountain abound in those writings. The pictures are attractive but are they true?

The census of 1880 shows (and the figures for 1880 are approximately correct for 1883) that in the strictly pastoral region embraced within the lines of New Mexico, Colorado, Wyoming, Dakota, Montana, Nevada, Utah, Washington, and Oregon there were 1,923,148 cattle or 416,573 less than in the state of Kansas and Nebraska. States that extend from Missouri river westward into the arid grazing belt, graze more cattle than all the so-called country excepting Texas. Colorado has been puffed up more extensively than any other State as a desirable location for cattle breeder. For years cattle have been driven from Texas to Colorado. In 1880 there were 346,739 cattle in Colorado. South Carolina a state never spoken of as cattle country possessed 363,709 cattle in 1880. Arkansas where the men are falsely supposed to spend their time lying in wait behind corn cribs for their personal foes contained 708,243 cattle or 351,504 more than Colorado. In 1880 Florida grazed 467,370 cattle over 120,000 more than Colorado.

The cattle country contains not including Texas about 800,000 square miles. The fact that buffaloes once grazed over most of the land is strongly dwelt upon by the cattle breeder. Throughout this vast range cattle are expected to pick up their living during the winter. It is asserted that the loss of stocks is very small on these natural breeding grounds. With all these advantages the cattle States do not graze as much stock as New York a state containing but 47,000 square miles and where the cattle are fed hay and grain for six months every year. The losses In New York by freezing and starving will not equal the loss in any of the cattle states of the far West. In one blizzard in the latter portion of the winter.

All men who have travelled over the Colorado plains know that that country is fully stocked with cattle. Many well informed men assert that the southern portion of the State that borders on the Arkansas river is overstocked and that the grass has been greatly injured by close feeding and the stock travelling over is as they walked to add fro from the uplands to the river for water. Wyoming, Dakota, and Montana are not fully stocked. Still the cattle have been driven out of some portions of those comparatively new and ungrazed ranges notably from the Laramie plains in Wyoming though in this case it is certain that the pressure exerted by the sheep herders had a marked influence on the cattle owners.

    Cattle raising in the West is life on the frontier. It is a life of ceaseless monotony. There is but little danger of the Indians being attracted away from Government rations in search of scalps. The extinction of the buffalo before the rifles of the white robe hunters has solved the Indian question. The ranges that these animals used to migrate over to and fro are now cattle ranges over which the stock growers ride. There is nothing fascinating in the life of a cowboy, or in that of an owner of a small herd. It can be summed up in a few weeks' hard riding in the spring, during the branding roundup, and a few weeks more riding during the beef roundup in the fall. The rest of the year is spent in watching the horns of cattle grow, in counting the rings on the base of those weapons of defence, and in cooking and eating bacon and bread. This attractive life is varied by men who have families and sufficient means by living in some little squalid frontier town. Life in one of these towns is not attractive. The men loaf. Time hangs heavily on the hands of such men as cannot supply themselves with intellectual amusement by sitting on an empty dry goods box and pounding their boot heels against the resounding sides, while discussing bucking ponies and cows whose tails have frozen off. These idle stock growers are apparently wrapped up in absorbing thought as to the price of cattle at the distribution points in the Eastern

States, or as to whether Clark's banana-tailed one-horned cow, the one with the diamond R brand on her right side and an under crop on her left ear, is seven or eight years old. There is some hunting done by these men, but the greater portion of them do not hunt. They loaf, they sleep, they lie on blankets, and they eat poor food wretchedly cooked. A bright nervous, intellectual young man would abandon his business, as it is generally conducted, in less than a week. He would turn his horse's head toward the nearest railroad station, and getting on the first train, would abandon ranch, cattle, horses and the log cabin standing on the sircoro-swept plain, and hasten to his father and confess that he had made a mistake. He would frankly acknowledge that he could not live without the society of his fellows.

The phrase "It is cattle country" means much more than Eastern Men suppose. To Western men and by Western I mean west of the 100th meridian, it conveys the impression of a country of extreme aridness, of rolling streams of alkaline water. Across the plains waves of heat roll in the summer causing the air to tremble, and through which medium all objects are distorted to the vision. In the winter artic storms sweep out of the north. The snow flies horizontally through the air. The furious wind drives it into ravines, there not being enough vegetation on the levels to hold the snow particles. In cattle country there are no trees, or good water, unless in mountain valleys. The grass becomes brown and dry in late June or early July. Every drop of rain that falls after the grass has died for want of water, injures the feed by washing nutriment out of it. This early death of the grass is to strangers in an airy manner. The cattle breeder indicates an extensive scope of arid country with outstretched sweeping arm, and says: "No need for mowing machines here. Nature makes the hay. No heavy work for men in providing feed for cattle during the winter. The grass cures where it grew. The cattle help themselves." The truth is that on the plains enough grass could not be grown in a hundred acres to feed a cow through the winter. In the valleys grass can be grown if the land is irrigated. And better hay — that is, more nutritious hay — made than any of the Eastern states. In twenty weeks more there is a crop of pigs. In less than a year from the date on which the farmers were satisfied that the corn crop would prove to be a fair one, the new crop of hogs are butchered in Chicago Kansas City. The stock of hogs can in a year be increased form scarcity to oversupply. Just as soon as this occurs, down goes the price of pork, until it is cheaper than beef, and millions of people who depend on their daily labor for their food, buy the cheaper meat. Beef is neglected. To sell it the price has to be reduced. If falls in price until it is comparatively as cheap as pork. This has been the history of all high prices of beef. A full corn crop reduces the price of meats. The bottom will fall out of the present price of meats. The bottom will fall out of the present excitement about cattle raising promptly after the husking of the first full crop of corn. Another factor that will aid in reducing the price of beef is the fact that no calves are killed in corn country. In many of the towns lying along the railroad in Kansas, Nebraska, Iowa, and Missouri, it is impossible to buy veal. The butchers say that they cannot purchase calves from the farmers.

The mortality among cows is very large on all ranges of high altitude. This is necessarily so under the present system of management. Two-year heifers drop calves in the early spring. An animal two years old has not read maturity. They shed their teeth at that age. The young creatures are called upon to fee strong calves running at their sides, to nourish others, and to complete their growth. The young animals apparently thrive until late in the summer. Then the calves are strong and demand more milk than their dams can supply when fed on dry grass that has had a portion of its strength washed out by the rains. The heifers could be saved if their owners would wean the calves and allow them to recruit before the icy blasts of winter sift through them: but this is seldom done. The calves stick to their dams until the unfueled systems of the cows can no longer supply milk. By this time the animals are mere bones encased in a rough hide. They are almost ready to lie down and die. They have lost all ambition, all desire to live. In the case of a mature cow the results are much the same. These animals are never in good condition unless the grass has been of unusual goodness and the winter exceedingly mile. Thousands of cows die every winter because their owners neglect to wean their calves. On the plains, the breeding stock of a herd rapidly disappears, but they don't disappear from the herd books.

It is not generally known, in fact I believe that it has never been published that the movement of young cattle has begun to tend westward. I hear a sniff of incredulous disbelief. The fact remains the same. Many of the cattle breeders of Wyoming and Colorado have agents in the real cattle country composed of Iowa, Missouri, Arkansas, and the eastern portions of the Indian Territory, Kansas and Nebraska. These agents buy young cattle, chiefly steers which they ship to the Western ranges to replenish herds. These Eastern cattle are branded on their arrival in the West: but just how they appear on the books, none excepting the owners know. To those accustomed to placing confidence in magazine romances, this movement of young cattle looks like the importing of organ grinders into Italy. But it is a truth that should at once dissipate all glamour about the "great natural breeding ground." The stockmen have not been able to breed enough cattle to replenish their herds.

Since the settlement of Colorado and Wyoming thousands and thousands of Texas cows have been driven hither. The larger portion of the herds driven from Texas to the new countries are two and three year old heifers. They were hopefully expected to live for eight or ten years, and to form the foundations of herds form which hundreds of thousands of cattle should spring. Where the cows that were driven from the gramma and mesquite ranges of Texas? Their bones whiten the plains. Their flesh was eaten by wolves. They died from exposure in an Artic climate.

It must not be believed that all the land represented in bright colors on the maps of the land grant railroads are grazing lands. There are extensive tracts of land in the West that are remote from water. These are grassy deserts. There is a limit to the distance that horned stock can travel to and from a range for water. The daily drive of a herd of Texas cattle and they are by far the best travelers of all cattle is limited to fifteen miles. The animal will hold their flesh when travelling that distance per day. If pushed to twenty miles they rapidly lose flesh. This being so, it is plain that native cattle, that are notoriously poor travelers, cannot walk more than fifteen miles and keep in good condition. If the feeding grounds are more than eight miles from water, the cattle will not grow fat. If they are ten miles from water the animals will lose flesh. The limited capacity of stock to travel bars them from extensive ranges.

There is an act of Congress called the Desert Land act, under the provisions of which one 1,000 acres of land can be secured. The settler has to irrigate the tract, fence it and at the end of three years pay $1.25 per acre for it. It was supposed by the members of Congress from Eastern States that desert land would be reclaimed under this act. The trouble is that desert land is not taken, and the originators of the bill did not intend that lands actually desert would be taken. The plan is to claim the oasis of the plains, the natural meadows, to fence and irrigate them and thus get possession of the hay land, which in the future control the water, and through the water the hay lands and adjoining range. This process of absorbing the range can best be seen in the valley of the Arkansas River. There the river is fenced for miles and the process is complete. It can be seen in various stages of advancement in any of the Western Territories; in some but just commenced; in others almost finished. This law was devised by the cattle men for the purpose of defrauding the Government out of public grazing lands. Cunningly devise, it answers perfectly. The hay lands of the plains and mountain valleys will soon be in the possession of the men owning large herds.

Certain men, who have been successful in cattle raising, are seized by the coat collar and dangled before the eyes of Eastern public as remarkable examples of what industry and paying close attention to horned stock will accomplish for any young man who has the pluck to go West and work faithfully. If the stories are to be believed, these successful men always came West penniless. They arrived at certain towns astride a spavined, ringboned horse. This animal they traded for a spotted heifer. This heifer is represented as the foundation of the herd. They worked and every cent they earned they put into female cattle. Gradually they became rich. That is the regulation tale. The truth is that they invested considerable money in cattle. They branded all the calves they could catch. When their herd was filled with steers fit for the butcher, they opened a butcher shop in the nearest town and drove the other butchers, who did not own herds of cattle to despair by the low price of the beef they have sold and finally drove them out of business. This accomplished they promptly increased the price of beef until there was 500 per centrum profit in it. They kept the price up until the other shops resumed. They kept the price up until the other shops resumed business. Then down went the price of beef, until the other butchers could not afford to dull their knives and saws in cutting roasts and steaks. Again they shut up their shops. That very instant the black leg and kindred diseases broke out in the Eastern States, and skyward went the price of beef. For fourteen years I have seen this game played in the West. Another exceedingly profitable branch of the cattle business was and is, the supplying of Indians with beef. An Indian beef contract is a prize: it is a fortune for any Western Cattle Breeder. A thin scalawag Texan steer, that has been reduced by hard driving and alkaline water until it is doubtful if he will tip the scales at 600 pounds staggers off the platform under the weight of 1,300 pounds of beef. It is astonishing how heavy a steer is when an employee of the Department of the Interior weighs him.

As the business of cattle breeding ages, it tends to separate into different branches. At present some of the men who handle stock on the high plains refuse to own any cows. They have tried raising cattle and abandoned it as unprofitable. These men procure three-year steers from Oregon and Washington. These animals are bought in the early spring and are slowly drive to the Wyoming or Colorado ranges, arriving there in October. They are turned loose on the range and allowed to shift for themselves. In my opinion this is the safest branch of the cattle business. The young steers have not obtained their full growth. They are hearty and strong. It is seldom that any of them die. They are held over the winter and until next fall. They grow in size and weight and of course in value.

Another branch of the business is the fattening of cattle on hay. Again, three-year old steers are selected. They are driven into a corral, and there get all the hay they can eat. The mountain hay is so nutritious that the steers become as fat as corn-fed animals in the Eastern States. It is has been the custom for several years to ship beef during the winter when cattle are thin on the range, from Kansas City to Denver. The beef so shipped is of a good quality. This spring I saw better beef — that is fatter beef —hanging in a butcher shop in Laramie Wy., than I saw in Denver. This choice beef was hanging in a butcher shop was fattened on hay cut on the Little Laramie River. The business of winter feeding steers on the plains promises to increase rapidly in the near future. It is a perfectly safe business, and very profitable. As it increases, so will the value of hay lands obtained under the Desert Land act.

**FRANK WILKERSON**

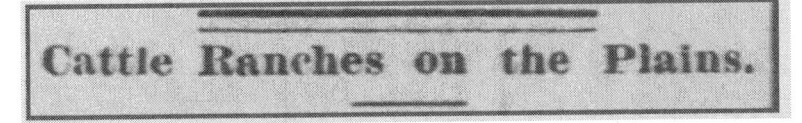

## Cattle Ranches on the Plains.

*Newton Kansan* **(Newton, Harvey, Kansas) 16 Aug 1883**. — Frank Wilkenson, "formerly of Kansas," has written a letter to the New York Sun on the cattle ranches of the far West, in which he asserts that the stories of fortunes to be made in cattle raising, beyond the

100th meridian, have little or no foundation in fact. He presents, to sustain his assertion, statistics showing that the vast herds ranging over the prairies of New Mexico, Colorado, Wyoming, Dakota, Montana, Washington, Oregon, Nevada and Utah exist only in the imagination of magazine writers who do not know a Durham steer from a scalawag Texan, or of ranchmen who wish to deceive capitalists. The territory embraced in the districts named reaches 300,000 square miles. The cattle quartered on it number, according to the last census, which holds good for to-day, 1,923,143, or 416,573 less than in the State of New York alone. Colorado especially has been puffed as a cattle raising State, but in 1880 Colorado had 340,739, or almost 20,000 less than South Carolina, which has no status whatever as a breeders' paradise.

This "cattle country" has few cattle Mr. Wilkenson contends, simply because it cannot support the millions and millions of horned animals with which popular imagination has stocked the vast plains beyond the borders of Nebraska and Kansas. The furious heats of summer scorch the grasses which are supposed to grow with tropical luxuriance. The rigid storms of winter sweep over the plains and freeze every living thing that cannot endure the rigors of an Arctic winter. Water is a rare article, and that which may be found is poor, and involves much traveling on the part of the cattle to reach. When they have to go more than eight miles to quench their thirst, they loose[7] flesh. When they have to rely entirely upon the dried grass for

---

[7] It is spelled "loose" rather than "lose" in the letter.

their winter food, they are likely to fare poorly, and, in multitudes of instances, die. The rain which falls up on this grass after the heats of June and July have made it hay, extracts large amount of its nourishment. Its lack of nutrition, added to the storms of winter, tell a story which may be read to the whitening bones bestrewing the plains after a severe season.

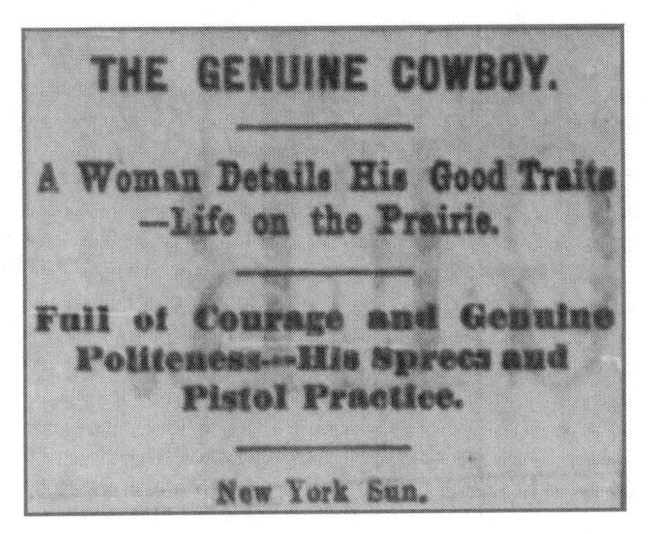

## THE GENUINE COWBOY.

### A Woman Details His Good Traits —Life on the Prairie.

### Full of Courage and Genuine Politeness—His Sprees and Pistol Practice.

*New York Sun.*

***Public Ledger*** **(Memphis, Tennessee) 30 Aug 1883.** — A letter from a cowboy's wife, from Benkleman, Neb. says, "I have been reading Frank Wilkeson's letters from Medicine Bow range and I find them very interesting and a trifle amusing. I have lived on a ranch for six years, I am the wife of cowboy. I see hundreds of cowboys yearly. I talk with them, observe their ways and know their habits, their modes of dress and their style of speech. Cowboys are universally proclaimed to be all that is bad and cruel. I say it is not so. Your correspondent asks: 'Is it a matter of surprise that cowboys are cruel, are brutal?' He includes all cowboys. If anyone should say that all negroes are villains because one of that race assaulted Miss Slocum near Salem, N. Y, a short time ago, his communication would be considered utterly devoid of sense. Why not say that all divines are unworthy to be called divines because a few of them fall from grace? Would it not be as just and right to say that all our Presidents are cheats because one man occupied the Presidential chair by fraud, or that all editors are liars because some have been found guilty of libel? I say no.

### HIS INNOCENT SPORTS.

A cowboy goes into a town. He becomes intoxicated on bad whisky and grows merry and jolly and fires his pistol into the air for fun. Perhaps he grows vicious and brutal and fires his pistol promiscuously at chimneys and lamp posts or anything else he sees. A sheriff's posse surrounds him. The air is thick with bullets and buckshot. Cowboy returns the fire. He breaks a leg or an arm, or perhaps he kills the Sheriff. Sometimes he is riddled with bullets. Sometimes he is captured, given a fair trial and hanged. Well and good we say that he gets his just deserts and there we hope it will rest; but it does not. His whole outfit (in cowboy language, all the boys who worked with him, including the inoffensive cook) are branded as villains of deep a dye as the murderous offender himself.

A short time ago an affray occurred in Ogallala, Neb. A cowboy became senseless from drink. He fired his pistol right and left and frightened the town out of its wits. At the outset he intended to do damage to no body. The sheriff and his posse opened fire on him. He returned it and shot the Sheriff in the leg. Then he fled, followed by a number of armed men. They followed him to his camp, where he was captured while trying to catch a fresh horse on which to flee. But before he was taken the Sheriff's posse fired volley after volley into the camp, which was manned by a smooth faced boyish cook alone whose only weapon was a dishcloth, and whose only crime against mankind lay in dealing out indigestible biscuits and badly cooked meat and beans to the boys. He escaped harm, but had he been slain the brave posse would have carried back the news to the town that two villains had been captured, one dead and the other alive.

## WHERE THE BLAME BELONGS.

What your correspondent said about the cattle owners is true. They turn cattle loose on the prairies knowing well that some of them will succumb to starvation or die of thirst before the spring opens. They know too, that it is cheaper to lose some than to feed them all. Of the horror and shame of it enough cannot be said; but I say let the blame rest where it belongs on the Eastern owners, not on the men who are hired to do their work as they are told to do it. Frank Wilkeson speaks of "the brutes who live in log cabins." Now the real brutes live back in our Eastern cities in fine mansions, drinking wines, while the cattle dependent upon them are thirsting and; dying. Will I be forgiven if I say in charity, that their neglect is more the outgrowth of carelessness than "callousness of heart." As your correspondent calls it? The owners are seldom present when their cattle are dying, so it is strange that, not seeing their suffering, they are not impressed by it.

As for the wolves killing poor cows we think Mr. Wilkeson is mistaken about the "poor cow." In our experience, it is oftener the fat calf or yearling, or even fat cow that is over powered by the wolves. We have never heard of a "poor" cow being killed while there was a fat one on the range. Wolves know which makes the best meat as well as their biped superiors. I know of cowboys who have saved up their earnings and are now small cattle owners themselves, and I know not of one who has turned his cattle out to live if they can, die if they must, in the bitter winters of this altitude. In summer their cattle are kept in close herds and hay is secured and sheds built for their comfort in winter. My husband, who is a thorough cowboy, asserts, and proves his assertions by his actions. That he would rather sell some of his cattle every autumn and buy corn for the rest with the money than to let the same number die of starvation.

I am writing of Nebraska and Kansas cowboys as I have found them. However, they are pretty much the same all over the West. Here they make their beds as the one Mr. Wilkerson described, with the addition of a pillow. Most of the cowboys of my acquaintance have pillows, some of which are made of "prairie feathers" (grass).

My husband is of the latter sort, and need I say that thanks are due his wife for it?

## MANNERS.

A word now about the manners of the cowboy, as compared with the manners of the "tenderfoot." The cowboy is invariably polite to ladies. He is deferential to all. He reveres all and his manner shows it, whether they be richly dressed or meanly dressed. He takes off his hat when he enters your house, and he treats your with respect and deference. The finely dressed, finely educated, smart M.D's or lawyers and graduates of all sorts, called "tenderfoot" are far different. I have had them enter my house with a swagger, with hats cocked on the back of their heads, and they stand or sit in the middle of the room and squirt tobacco juice toward the door. It always fell short of the mark and besmeared the carpet. The majority of them seem to think that good manners permit them to enter lady's house and smoke in her presence without apology or asking leave. They invariably drawl out, "I should think ye get lonesome way out here?

## LIFE ON THE PRAIRIE.

I cannot tell how many times I have made answer to that question. I always answer that I never get lonesome. Then they look at me with an insipid sure, as much as to say: "Why did I waste that interesting, deeply thought out question on her? She does not know enough to get lonesome, she is contented with that cad of a husband, who wears a white hat with a leather band and leather leggings. She cannot see their fine points nor discover their desirable qualities. She would not feel at home in anything but a Godforgotten country, so why should I take my hat off in her presence or expectorate outside the door?"

So grows the puddle on the carpet. I can be excused for answering. I am perfectly contented and happy except when tenderfeet come round. Not more than one tenderfoot in ten acts as though he has been well brought up. They think they have found a place where manners and good breeding are unnecessary, and as they are not natural gifts to them, but purely assumed, they fall off easily when out of sight of their fine friends. When they tire of playing the role of gentlemen they should go among savages. If this catches the eye of any "tenderfeet" who are in our cattle country, or who contemplate coming here, I hope they will remember that gentlemen show respect to ladies wherever they meet them.

**AN EASTERN BUGABOO.**
We find the following paragraph in the Washington *National Republican:*

**The *Atchison Daily Champion* (Atchison, Atchison, Kansas) 19 Sep 1883.** — "Gov. Sheldon, of New Mexico, writes a beautiful letter to the Acting Secretary of the Interior, setting forth the great natural advantages of that territory, the happiness of the people, the splendid prosperity, the glorious future. But the Governor said nothing about the New Mexican cowboy, whose hip pocket bulges out as big as the hump on the back of the Arabian *camelus dromedarius*, and who carries in his left boot leg a knife as big as a handsaw. Gov Sheldon should, not have omitted this attraction. It is the bullwhacker of the prairies who makes the southwest so beautiful and sadly romantic."

The above portrays common, but hardly excusable, ignorance. A scribe who does not comprehend the difference between a "bullwhacker" and a "cowboy," ought not to attempt the description of "wild Western scenes." A "bullwhacker" is a teamster, who walks along the road beside a string of steers or bulls, and recites to them fragmentary passages of the Scripture and enforces his commentary with a big whip. A "cowboy" is rarely seen on the ground, but sticks on a pony till his (cowboy's) legs come to look like a pair of hames. His business is to drive cattle from one point to another, or to watch them on the range, and round them up and brand them, and perform all and several the little offices necessary for their good.

About this same cowboy there is a deal of nonsense published in the Eastern papers. He is by no means the desperate creature he is painted. He is not by any means a "holy terror" in New Mexico; he is, on the other hand, one of the best and bravest citizens of that country. It is evident that the Washington City man, who does not know a "cowboy" from a "bullwhacker," cannot distinguish between a "cowboy" and a "rustler." Now, a "rustler" is a bad subject, and the peaceable, quiet, law-abiding people of New Mexico, "cowboys" included, have had much trouble in hunting down, shooting and hanging these villainous "rustlers." It is evident the Republican editorial writer has confounded the "rustler" with the "cowboy," a mistake we would not advise him to make in the "cowboy's" presence.

The "cowboy" carries his revolvers though in the best Western society a revolver is known as a "gun," and occasionally he "turns her (the gun) loose," but he shoots only those who are "on the shoot." He who taketh up the "gun" shall fall by the "gun;" but the peace able man, who is not on blood intent could live forever in harmony with the "cowboy," provided he could reconcile himself to the same form of bowel burning fluid that the cowboy drinks.

The "cowboy" occasionally "takes the town," but it is usually one of the towns that like to be taken; in short, the "cowboy" is very like the sailor on shore, or soldier out on a lark. Many wickednesses are attributed to him of which he is not guilty; the criminals are the "rustlers," men who have never been "cowboys." One of the worst "wolves" we have ever had in Kansas was once a railroad engineer.

We think the sages of the Eastern press will have to brush up on the "cowboy." They evidently need information, as their ignorance leads them in the direction of injustice.

> **A Letter from a Cowboy.**
>
> TO THE EDITOR OF THE SUN—*Sir:* A communication from a cowboy will, I think, be something new to the columns of THE SUN.

**The *Sun* (New York, New York) 2 Oct 1883**. — I have never written a letter for publication and consequently have very grave doubts regarding my ability as a writer; but I have sufficient audacity to induce me to make an effort. Being only an unsophisticated cowboy, your many readers need not expect anything brilliant from me. On the contrary, I intend to write a very plain letter.

I have been a cowboy for several years I was born and raised in the East. Not too well raised you know or I would not be punching cattle now away out in this half civilized section of the country and leading the lonely, unloved and unloving life that I do. There are quite a number of cowboys who were born in the East and came West with their parents their infancy in search of homes and there are those who were born on the range and raised in the saddle. Again there are cowboys like myself who were raised East and sent West by misfortune. The life a cowboy leads is not void of danger and is calculated to make him wild, daring and fearless. There is a fascination in the life which I cannot describe. He often sleeps out on the range in wet and cold with only one or two pairs of blankets. His food consist almost entirely of bread of his own make, bacon and beans, and strong black coffee. I consider myself a man of some taste and refinement yet being poor I'd rather be a cowboy than an employee in some other business.

I have frequently read of evil but very seldom read of good or noble acts committed by cowboys yet were the truth known I think the latter would outnumber the former. It's a fact that Eastern people consider cowboys a half savage ignorant set of beings without considering that it takes all kinds of people to make a world or that there are exceptions to every rule.

When a "tenderfoot" comes West and is by chance thrown into the company of cowboys he carries himself in a dignified lordly way or else he acts as though he were among wild beasts and feared to excite their anger. This simply disgusts the cowboys and while some openly show their contempt others maintain a polite Indifference.

I'll conclude my letter by repeating a story which was told by cowboy one night in camp while I was with an outfit on the trail with beeves for the Eastern markets. There were half a dozen of us sitting around the camp fire. Several songs had been sung and story telling finally became chief pastime. One of the boys related the following: A rather timid young man from the East was travelling through the West by stage and after asking the stage driver a great many questions about buffaloes bears and Indians he finally inquired If they would be likely to meet with any cowboys expressing a wish at the same time to see them if I they did. The driver replied that they would probably meet with some before reaching their destination. The young gentlemen proceeded to relate some of the lurid stories ho had read concerning cowboys and while he was telling one of the most thrilling yarns a party of cowboys returning from town dashed around a bend in the road firing their six-shooters and yelling like demons. Young Timid rolled off his seat into the bottom of the stage, and after the cowboys had passed rose up, pale and trembling and ejaculated, "Great God! They're part human, ain't they?"

The SUN shines brightly and casts its rays on every range and while my letter may not Interest all your readers it will least prove satisfactory to the cowboy fraternity.

 **SILVER CITY, N.M., Sept 24**    **R. B. JUNYOR.**

> THERE can be no objection, says the Cincinnati Times-Star, to an American citizen pasturing his cattle on the public domain, when the rights of others are not interfered with; but when foreign capitalists come over here, buy stock and cooly proceed to utilize the grass on government land, a protest would seem to be in order. A letter from Wyoming says three-fourths of the great herds of cattle now pasturing on public land in that territory are owned in England. Wouldn't it be the proper thing for Uncle Sam to require these Englishmen to either settle in this country or pay rent?

The *Kinsley Mercury* (Kinsley, Kansas) 27 Oct 1883.

## The Wyoming Cowboys.

The cowboy has been seen by a correspondent of the Pittsburg *Commercial*, who writes from Carbon county, Wyoming: We found him first at Rawlings at night, and he seemed to be slightly on a tear. He was across the street in a saloon, imbibing Territorial lightning at twenty-five cents a drink. He was fast whooping it up with "the boys," and, as steam rose in the flues of his boiler, he gave vent to shrill and sharp warwhoops. After weeks, or possibly months, on the range or trail he collects his pay—from $10 to $50 a month—and goes to the nearest trading post and "blows in" his hard earnings, first taking pains to buy the finest "flop hat," a white felt with a broad brim, the neatest-fitting boots, the brightest silk handkerchiefs, and spurs with rowels as big as a blacking-box lid. Then, after shedding his old toggery, he is ready for "a fly" with any of the boys who may be in town for the same purpose.

The *Daily Republican* (Monongahela, Pennsylvania) 8 Nov 1883.

# Chapter 5: 1884

*"Several of the cowboys pronounced her a "thoroughbred" and a "long horn" — their choicest compliments, for, in the fertile vocabulary of the cowboy the terms "half breed" and "short horn" are equivalent to the "tenderfoot" or days gone by, with, perhaps a shade more of derision to them."*

-The Boston Globe, 1884.

## Cowboys.

*New Ulm Review* (New Ulm, Minnesota) 16 Jan 1884. — The "cowboys" of the Rocky mountain regions are a race or a class peculiar to that country. They have some resemblance to the corresponding class on the southern side of the Rio Grande, but are of a milder and more original type. In the great herding districts, where the cattle are fattened in great part upon the public domain, and roam, winter and summer, over vast areas without fences, without roads, and with only scattered and irregular places for water and shelter, the herdsmen play an important industrial role. It is their business to keep the cattle as nearly together as possible to guide them to the springs and wooded hollows, to separate them when they get mixed up with those of other droves, to brand them at the proper seasons, and to drive them to the nearest market at others. Often their regular occupation is attended with a good deal of danger. In Montana and in some parts of Colorado and Dakota, the Indians, turned loose to hunt buffalo near their reservations, fall upon the cattle and run them off, and against these raids the "cowboys" go always armed, and not unfrequently have to undertake exploits which, were they United States cavalrymen, would be reported to the War Department as "battles." At other times the men in the employ of rival and jealous owners become involved in quarrels which end in a more or less free fight. Again, when the season is severe and snow falls among the lower slopes of the mountains, the care of the herds becomes a hazardous task. Still again the half-tamed cattle "stampede," and it becomes a matter of no small amount of courage, skill and address to keep them or get them together. On such occasions the "cowboys" are obliged to hang on the flanks of the plunging herd and keep them, as far as they can, headed in the same direction, until the cattle from sheer weariness lapse into some sort of quiet and orderliness. The tendency to "break" is a mastery even to the most experienced herders. It usually shows itself toward night, and there are unmistakable signs of its approach, but no general theory of its origin has been reached.

  The outfit of the cowboy is a horse, usually one of the "ponies" of the region — swift, tough, ugly in look and temper, but capable of good service when once trained, a Mexican or "army" saddle, such as are shipped in great quantities from New York, a blanket, or, with the test herdsmen, a pair, one being of rubber, one or more pistols, sometimes a rifle, and with great uniformity, a liberal flask of whisky. Among those who seek this wild life on the very frontiers of civilization, or beyond them, there are naturally many untamed and lawless spirits, and these have given to the name of cowboy a character hardly deserved by the class. For the most part they are laborious, faithful and as sober as their fellow-men in the same region. But constant exposure, a monotonous life varied only by danger or exertion of extraordinary character, and exclusion from the usual social relations, inevitably tend to make the more disorderly among them reckless and cruel. Gambling and drinking are about the only diversions accessible, and both are indulged in with a zest quite unknown to the quieter circles of civilized parts of the country. Even among the worst "cowboys" thieving is rare, and the outrages with which they are charged in this line are usually committed by men who resemble them only in being mounted and armed. There attaches to the name an unconscious association with the cowboys of the Revolution, whose only calling was to steal cattle and everything else they could and run off from either side along the "debatable ground" between the British and Continental camps. The cowboys of the west have, on the contrary, a regular business, which the greater number of them follow with quite a much fidelity as the average farm hand or "drover" of the east.

It is not to be denied, however, that the exceptions to this rule are sufficiently striking to attract the attention of the lovers of the picturesque in current reading newspaper or other. Occasionally a band of the cowboys will take it into their heads, in an interval of leisure, to "clean out" a neighboring town. For one of these excursions they "load up," with whisky, gallop at nightfall into the streets, and race down them, firing right and left at any one whose appearance indicates a degree of luxury which, in the interest of their ideal democracy, should be suppressed. Then they visit the liquor saloons or gambling halls, which are only too frequent, consume what they like, and drive out the occupants. A few weeks ago a squad of five rode into Ute Creek, Colorado, and perceiving a Mexican trader with the name Don Macedio Arragon, made some impudent demand of him. He refused it, snatched his shotgun and retreated down the road. When the cowboys followed and fired on him he returned the fire, killed two of them and wounded a third, and then fell, shot in four places. He lingered twelve hours and died, and the murderers escaped. At Deadwood a band recently undertook to "clean out" a Mexican gambling saloon, but two of them were killed, and the others fled. On a lonely ranch in Colorado a little company of them quarreled over their cards. In the first moment the oil lamp was thrown down, and a desperate fight with knives and pistols went on in the darkness, until four men were left lifeless on the floor, slippery with blood, only one escaped, badly gashed and shot, to tell the awful tale. Terrible as are the are the incidents of a mode of life which necessarily draws many of the more wayward and violent of the frontier population, and though they stand out in bolder relief they are not proofs of a greater brutality or a lower type of manhood than the affrays which frequently take place on the excursion boats from our own city. Indeed bad as are the worst of cowboys, the class, as a whole, are better than the "gangs" which infest portions of the river wards of New York, the neighborhood of the Thames Embankment in London, or the *quartiers accentriques* of Paris. And what is more, the worst of the former are sure to disappear, while the latter grows in number and violence with the progress of "civilization."

## THE "ROUND-UP."

### The Special Laws and Customs Protecting Cattle-Raisers.

Gathering the Herds at the "Round-Up"---Branding the Calves and Selling the "Mavericks"---Facts and Figures.

[Colorado Letter.]

The *Topeka Daily Capital* (Topeka, Kansas) 08 Apr 1884. *Catoctin Clarion* (Mechanicstown, Maryland) 24 Apr 1884. — Although a great deal has been written of late years upon the important subject of cattle raising on the plains and in the parks and valleys of Colorado, comparatively little is really known of this business outside of those actually engaged in it. Owing to the peculiar nature of the industry special laws and customs prevail regarding its protection. The cattle are placed on ranges which may or may not belong to their owners, in fact, these ranges are most generally wild government land and are sometimes of enormous extent. This involves the necessity for the employment of a large number of horses and men to properly cover the extent of territory over which the cattle roam. The liability of confusion in a property as wandering in its nature as this makes it necessary for the different owners to use many devices and precautions to identify and protect their property and to adopt rules and regulations for their own government, which it would be almost impossible to put in a statute book, but which are recognized by all of the courts as equitable and just and as binding upon the parties concerned as though enacted by the regular law-making authorities. These latter include the system of round-ups, branding of calves, regulations regarding the disposition of unclaimed calves separated from their mothers called "mavericks," and also those designed to detect cattle stealing.

## THE ROUND UP DISTRICTS

In order to carry out thoroughly the system, it has been found necessary in every state to form in each round-up district Cattle Growers associations, in addition to which each state and territory where the cattle industry occupies a prominent position, has its state organization. In Colorado, there are seventeen round-up districts whose associations meet twice each- year and a state association which holds annual meetings. A large number of the regulations of these associations are incorporated as laws in the statute books of the state, among them those providing for state cattle inspectors and round-up commissioners. These officials are appointed by the governor at the suggestion and recommendation of the state association. The board of state inspectors consists of five prominent cattlemen, and "the round-up" commissioners consist of three from each district. Their duties are to see to it that all the state laws are enforced and association rules obeyed in their several districts, and to have a general supervision of the subjects of round-ups, branding of calves and gathering and transporting beef.

## GATHERING THEM IN.

The busy times are confined to the roundup seasons, of which there are normally two, although the first, which begins about May 20 and continues until June 1, and the second commencing some three weeks later, and continuing well into August, are so nearly together that they might well be called one season. At these round-ups, certain designated men, accompanied by a foreman or captain, start from some given point and travel over all the ranges in their district. They take with them wagons containing supplies sufficient for their probable stay, and the brands of every owner in the district. As the work is, very severe upon the horses, especially in "cutting out" from the herd, each man has from six to eight horses, riding one, herding the others and driving them along with the wagons. In active work a horse should be changed every three or four hours, and the rider, when he feels that his animal is exhausted, rides up to the herd, lassoes another, and quickly changing the saddle, and sets his tired horse free. At the round-up all the cattle in the district are gathered together in one vast herd and driven to the rendezvous near the center of the district. The work of identification and branding the calves then begins. The ownership of the calves is ascertained from the brand of the mother, and a similar brand is placed upon the offspring.

### "MAVERICKS."

It happens, however, that in numerous instances the calves become separated from their mothers, and it is a matter of impossibility to ascertain their owners. These strays are called "mavericks," and become the joint property of the association of the round-up district in which they are found. These mavericks are, by a rule of the Colorado associations, sold to the highest bidders among their members at the end of the season, and the proceeds paid in the general fund provided for the maintenance of the organization. The receipts thus realized frequently amount to the handsome sum of from $3,000 to $5,000 per year in each district. At the second later round-up the same branding process is carried out, and the additional feature of gathering beef is added. This consists of selecting such cattle as are in desirable condition for shipment and may include all of the different brands. An inventory is made or the cattle so selected and a copy forwarded to the different inspectors and agents along the line of route the cattle will be driven or carried to market, as well to the parties to whom they are con-signed. When the cattle are gathered and the branding of the calves completed, the work of separating the herds begins and the difficult task of placing the cattle of each brand in separate herds is accomplished. These are then driven to their proper ranges by the herders.

## CATTLE DETECTIVES.

The round-up party, which, is in considerable numbers, is generally accompanied by a man or men from each surrounding district and from the adjacent states and territories who are furnished with all the brands of their districts or states, and who are present for the purpose of identifying cattle which may have strayed from the ranges of other districts. Owing to, the seeming facility with which this class of property might be stolen the greatest precautions are taken, of course, to prevent cattle stealing and to this end the police and inspection service is rendered as nearly perfect as possible. There are employed in Colorado alone upwards of thirty stock inspectors or detectives who are constantly traveling over the state, examining hides in butchering establishments and inspecting brands, especially at shipping points. Their operations, however, are not confined to this state alone, but extend to all points whence cattle are shipped. Some are stationed at Kansas City, Omaha, Pacific Junction on the Burlington & Missouri, and other points on the routes to market. These men exercise the right to examine all manifests and compare them with the brands of the cattle shipped, and the lists which they have with them. If they discover in the shipment different brands from those on the manifests, they cause the arrest of the shipper, if they believe the animals stolen, otherwise they demand and receive payment for the strange brand and turn over the amounts so received to the proper owners, so that with an honest enforcement of this rule cattle stealing is next to impossible.

## ITEMS OF INTEREST.

The cattle in Colorado are owned by about 800 men who have in their employment perhaps 3,000 herders to care for them. The wages of these men average from $35 to $40 per month and board, and for foremen $100 to $125 per month. The number of men required to care for the herds varies in proportion according to the size of the herd. One of 20,000 would require about twenty-two herders, 10,000 about fifteen herders, 5,000 about ten herders, 2,500 about seven herders and 1,000 about four herders, so that the larger herds entail less expense proportionately than the smaller ones. The total cost of herding 20,000 or upwards per head 50 cents per year, 10,000 and upwards 75 cents, and a less number $1.00 per head. A number of improved breeds are being crossed with Texas stock, and the results are always satisfactory. These include the Poll Angus, Short Horns and Galloways; of these Colorado men just now prefer the former, but the fashion in cattle changes as it does in bonnets.

## TOO MUCH FOR THE COWBOY.

### A Colorado Pugilist Takes the Wind Out of a Boaster from Wyoming.

[Fort Fetterman Cor. New York Sun.]

The *Wilkes-Barre News* (Wilkes-Barre, Pennsylvania) 03 Dec 1884. — The cowboys do not have any such fun as they used to have, but those who make their headquarters in this neighborhood have been enjoying themselves a good deal of late. Some time ago the boys had nothing to do for six months in the year. Now they are "busy nearly all the time." First comes the general round-up, then the calf round-up, then haying, then the beef round-up, then the gathering in of bulls and weak cows, and finally a winter of feeding hay. Many of the old-time cowboys in this section resented the idea of making hay, and some of them quitted the business in disgust when asked to go into the field for that purpose. One of the dissatisfied members of the fraternity was Alex Thebold, a man who considered himself one of the toughest on the range. He made a good deal of fun of the haymakers, and whipped a few of them in fist fights when they undertook to reply to his taunts. After a while he got a reputation as a pugilist, and one man after another whom he encountered was polished off in fine style.

"I will teach you tenderfeet and haymakers a new art," he said, "In our day we shot and shot to kill, but it will never do for you to try that on. Don't you fool with the weapons? Learn to defend yourselves with the fists. That is all you will ever need. Put away your guns and I'll show you how the thing is done.

After he had whipped every cowboy in the camp and found himself too big for the company he was in, someone suggested that he ought to go out into the states and travel on his muscle. Everybody agreed that that was the proper thing to do. He had gained all the glory he could among the cowboys, and all that he now lacked was recognition outside. He fell in with the idea very quickly and some of the boys, seeing a chance to get him into trouble proposed that a subscription be taken up to take him to Denver, and prepare him for a match with a local bruiser. He assented to the scheme, and a few days ago, accompanied by four or five of the boys, he left for that city.

Once there Thebold announced himself as the cowboy knocker, and claimed that he could whip anything that went on two feet. The city sports him over, pronounced him good and persuaded Johnny Clow, the champion of Colorado, to make a match with him. The cowboys put up the money for Thebold and one night last week was selected for the mill, the place chosen being a base ball park on the outskirts of the town. The men and their backers proceeded thither at midnight. The moon was shining, and it was light enough to see pretty well

While the seconds were arranging the preliminaries the cowboys began to hope Alex would not kill the other fellow at the first blow.

"Oh, I won't murder him," Thebold said confidently, "but I'll show him what kind of battering rams they raise on Crazy Woman's creek. I'll just spoil him, and then call for another one. I don't want to use up all my fun in a minute."

When time was called the Colorado champion man jumped into the ring quietly and Thebold bounded in with an air of defiance. They shook hands, and then the cowboy began to dance up and down. Pretty soon he made a terrific lunge at Clow and struck him a stinging blow on the nose, drawing blood, but leaving his own head unguarded. Clow was staggered for an instant by the suddenness and force of the blow, but recovering himself, he hit the cowboy a crusher on the left ear and followed it up as quick as lightning with another bone breaker on the neck. Thebold sat down, got up, walked around a little, holding his head in both hands, and trying to assume a perpendicular position, and then said: "Boys, I believe that cuss has broken my neck. He's just one too many for me on this round-up. Take me home."

All hands tried their best to persuade him to try it again, but he resolutely refused. "I'm not very well, and I didn't suppose you had any such knockers as that fellow is. I'm going back to Fetterman." The boys brought him home, and since then half a dozen of them have whipped him and others are coming in to try their hands.

## THE COWGIRL OF TEXAS.

Miss Marie Bynum and Her Rare Accomplishments—Pronounced a "Thoroughbred" and "Long Horn" by All the Gallant Boys, and Presented with a Gold Ring for a Testimonial.

[New York Sun.]

The *Boston Globe* (Boston, Massachusetts) 22 Dec 1884. — MIDLAND, Tex., December 10. There is an ocean of prairie about this new town, and it rises and falls as far as the eye can reach like the swell of a troubled sea. With a strong glass one can see in the distance a mass of sheep tended by a lonely shepherd, in a yellow "slicker" or oil-skin ulster, and a black Spanish shepherd dog. Herds or antelope following a leader scamper across the plains, stirring up flocks of Mexican quail and prairie chickens, and causing excitement in the prairie dog towns where the fat rodents plunge head first into their holes and then stick out their heads to see what startled them. Like a dark cloud on the horizon, great herds of cattle appear in the distance, either in motion or under the guard of cowboys holding them. The herd of Colonel A. W. Dunn, president of the Colorado National Bank, came upon the plains the other day, and the colonel came here when his niece, Miss Marie Bynum of Mississippi, to "cut out," as the phrase goes, the beeves that were ready for market, and to pen them in the cattle-pens at the railroad station. The wild Texas steers were full of life and run, and the cowboys had their hands full, with all of their skill, to get them penned. Colonel Dunn, who is a typical cowman, mounted a mustang to help the cowboys, and his niece insisted upon going with him. She could not he persuaded that there was any danger in the adventure, or that her dress and sex placed her at any disadvantage in at effort for when the cowboys were rigged with Mexican spurs, big leather leggings, three or four revolvers, lariats at their saddle horns big white sombreros with rattlesnake skins twisted about them, and watch chains of snake rattles. She insisted that if she could get a swift pony and a side saddle she would show that she could ride alongside of the wildest steer and turn him, in spite of his dangerous horns. The pony was provided, and Miss Bynum, placing her foot in the hand of a cowboy, leaped into the saddle, and gathering up the reins, dashed off with a hearty laugh, followed by her escort of cowboys, who spun over the prairie after her. She reined up as they came into the herd. As the process of selection of the beeves required a quick judgment that only experience gives.

The cowboys went into the herd, and their trained ponies, when they were pointed to steers that were to be "cut out," ran them out of the herd, and, as soon as a bunch was formed, the cowboys swung around them and Miss Bynum, with a lash made of the end of the reins, started her pony forward and joined in the semi-circle, and started tile steers to the pen. The work was exciting to a novice, and the fair cowgirls cheeks flushed as she sped along. A big brown steer, all branded over, reared up, and, breaking out of the line, tossed his horns and his tail up, and started off like a deer. Miss Bynum whirled her pony and started after the animal. She did her work bravely. The cowboys watched her with admiration. Her pony dashed alongside of the steer, and the cowboys expected thee as the animal turned, he would eaten his horns in her drapery, or she would plunge over the pony's head as he turned with the steer. They saw her stop as the steer turned and balance herself like a skilled equestrienne, and then head off the steer and turn him back. Soon she came dashing back alongside the steer and landed him in the bunch that was headed for the pen. Several of the cowboys pronounced her a "thoroughbred" and a "long horn" — their choicest compliments, for, in the fertile vocabulary of the cowboy the terms "half breed" and "short horn" are equivalent to the "tenderfoot" or days gone by, with, perhaps a shade more of derision to them.

Miss Bynum, when the first lot of cattle was penned dashed back to the herd, and, with a little instruction, began to help "cut out" the cattle. Each trip from the herd to the pen was marked by some exciting chase of a steer, and each time the young woman bore herself bravely, and she did not let a single steer escape. When at the pen, of which the cattle with apparent consciousness of their impending fate after the long trip to Chicago, showed fear, they tried hard to escape. With heads down, the steers that could would dart past the ponies and dash away, and the nearest cowboy would touch his spurs to the pony's side and point him and start on the chase. The wild Texas steers are swift-footed and it takes a good rider to pass one and turn him, but Miss Bynum was equal to every steer that invited her pony to a run. Although she was in imminent danger of being dragged off her mount by the horns of some steer striking into her riding habit, she was able to manage her skirts as well as her pony, and when the task was ended she contemplated the forest of horns in the cattle pen with sparkling eyes and rosy cheeks.

At night, when the cowboys were drinking their black coffee and eating their jerked buffalo meat, they agreed to present Miss Bynum with some token of their appreciation of her assistance, and a few days ago there came to the bank at Colorado a massive gold ring, inscribed "To Miss Bynum from the Texas cowboys." Colonel Dunn presented the sleeker circle of gold to his niece, and said that he hoped it would signify an engagement of her services at the annual round-up on the plains.

"I never enjoyed anything so much in my life," said Miss Bynum to the writer, "and, would you believe it? I didn't hear the cowboys quote Scripture once. I am going to ride on the next round-up, and I expect to do much better. I'll show them what a cowgirl can do."

# Photo Gallery

Branding calves on roundup. 1888[8].

Cowboys Eating Out on the Range, Chuck Wagon in Background. 1880.[9]

---

[8] Grabill, John C. H, photographer. "Branding calves on roundup". South Dakota, 1888. Photograph. https://www.loc.gov/item/99613914/ Library of Congress.

[9] Cowboys Eating Out on the Range, Chuck Wagon in Background. , ca. 1880. [Between and Ca. 1910] Photograph. https://www.loc.gov/item/2012646306/ Library of Congress.

Round-up scenes at Belle Fourche South Dakota, 1887.[10]

Cowboys, Roping a Buffalo on the Plains.[11]

---

[10] Grabill, John C. H, photographer. Round-up scenes on Belle Fouche sic in. Belle Fourche South Dakota, 1887. Photograph. https://www.loc.gov/item/99613911/ Library of Congress.

[11] Grabill, John C. H, photographer. Cowboys, Roping a Buffalo on the Plains. South Dakota, None. [Between 1887 and 1892] Photograph. https://www.loc.gov/item/99613915/ Library of Congress.

The Cowboy, 1888.[12]

Cowboys Roping Cow in Pasture, 1888.[13]

---

[12] Grabill, John C. H, photographer. "The Cow Boy" / J.C.H. Grabill, photographer, Sturgis, Dakota Ter. South Dakota, ca. 1888. Photograph. https://www.loc.gov/item/99613920/ Library of Congress.

[13] Watkins, Carleton E, photographer. Lakeside Ranch Lassoing a cow. California, 1888. Photograph. https://www.loc.gov/item/2009633196/ Library of Congress.

Cowboys roping a wolf, 1887.[14]

Cowboys catching horses.[15]

---

[14] Grabill, John C. H, photographer. "Roping gray wolf," Cowboys take in a gray wolf on "Round up," in Wyoming. Wyoming, 1887. Photograph. https://www.loc.gov/item/99613918/ Library of Congress.

[15] Grabill, John C. H, photographer. Roping and changing scene at --T Camp on round up of --T. 999 --S. & G., A.U.T. and others on Cheyenne River. Cheyenne River South Dakota, None. [Between 1887 and 1892] Photograph. https://www.loc.gov/item/99613917/ Library of Congress.

# Chapter 6: 1885

*"McGaigan exhibited to me the modus operandi of handling the rope, and some of his feats performed in my presence were not only executed with marvelous precision, but were also beautiful to look at."*

-Letter from Wyoming to Tennessee, 1885

—It is reported that Jay Usher and Jim Carney, of the town of Weston, Dunn county, were killed by Dakota cowboys, while en route to Dakota. The herders attacked the Usher-Carney party, believing them to be cattle thieves, and annihilated them, hanging several and shooting those who attempted to escape.

The *Neenah Daily Times* (Neenah, Wisconsin) 5 Jan 1885.

—A story came to me the other day of an engineering party in Dakota that had seated themselves at their dinner table in a tent, when a party of cowboys rode up. One of them dismounted, and thrusting his pistol in the middle of a rice pudding that was placed in the center of the table, called out: "Whoever wants pudding must ask me." No one seemed to care for dessert that day. —*Chicago Rambler.*

Crawford Mirror (Steelville, Missouri) · 8 Jan 1885

From a letter from Wyoming we learn of a singular and fatal accident that occurred at what is known as Hot Sulphur springs, on the Stinking Water on the 27th of January. It seems Thomas Hefron left Comte du Dore's ranch with the intention of going to the North Fork of the Stinking Water, and nothing more was seen or heard of him until the morning of the 29th, when his pack horse was found close to the ranch of Comte du Dore, which led to a fear that something had gone wrong, and a search being made his saddle horse was found tied to a large rock about 100 yards from the hot springs. On close examination his dead body was found in the hot water, where it had evidently been lying the from morning of the 27th until the morning of the 29th. It is supposed that he had gone in to bathe and was suffocated by the gas from the springs. The whereabouts of his relatives is unknown and any person that can give any information that will leading to find his former home will greatly oblige his friends in Wyoming by writing to M. C. Tracy, care Comte du Dore, Corbett, Wyoming.

The *Billings Herald* (Billings, Montana) 14 Feb 1885.

### The Boys from Hardman's Ranch.
### Wyoming Letter to Pittsburg Commercial.

*Harrisburg Telegraph* (Harrisburg, Pennsylvania) 21 Feb 1885. — On Tuesday of last week we had visitors. Six of the boys from Hardman's ranch descended on us like a wolf on the fold. They meant to stay, they said, until they had eaten us out. From the way they handled the dinner that day it looked as if their visit would be mighty short. As they brought sundry flasks of Western Kill-at-a-Hundred yards, they were received with open arms. After dinner everybody was feeling good, and the fun began. In our ranch house there are three rooms, kitchen, dining room and sleeping apartment. The walls of the dining room are covered every inch of them with pictures from illustrated papers. Worthies of all traces and condition lend their August presence to our meal, and beauties of all styles look down upon the admiring faces of the cow punchers. "Say, Hank," said the leader of the visitors to our cook, "that old duffer in the wig is too snide. Watch us bore him." Thereupon that irreverent herder pulled out his six shooter and shot Benjamin Franklin square in the eye. That opened the ball. Our foreman was away and our boys and the visitors did just as they pleased. The whole crowd began to blaze away at the pictures on the wall. There was a picture of Guiteau posted the kitchen door. I believe that every fellow in the room blazed away at him. "That pretty girl's nose is too long," one would say and then proceed to shave off pieces with his revolver. The ballot girls received special attention. After the shooting there was mighty little left of their scant clothing.

## War against Wild Horses.
### STOCKMEN ORGANIZING HUNTERS TO SHOOT THEM—SKILL AND PATIENCE REQUIRED TO CATCH THEM.

The *Wellsboro Gazette Combined with Mansfield Advertiser* (Wellsboro, Pennsylvania) 17 Mar 1885. — A letter from Cheyenne to the Chicago *Tribune* says that wild horses have become so numerous on the plains that some of the stockmen in that vicinity have organized a hunting party, whose object will be to thin them out. The hunters are provided with long-range rifles, fleet ponies, and supplies and forage enough to last winter, and they will endeavor to make a clean job of it. These horses have existed on the plains for many years, but of late they have been increasing very fast and are quick to scent the approach of foes, fleet as the antelope that may often be seen browsing in security at their side, and unmanageable as the wind. Native animals when turned loose on the prairie become wild, and if allowed to run without being disturbed breed very rapidly. Horses continually break away from their owners and join the wild horses and is the reason why stockmen are aroused over the subject. Men who crossed the plains in 1849 encountered many wild horses, and for years afterward, they have increased rather than diminished. Horses stand the winter much better than cattle and unless the weather is unusually severe will come out fat in the spring.

Every year large numbers of horses escape from the settlers. Some of them are found, but when mares escape they are never reclaimed. In wandering over the plains they encounter the wild bands, and from that time forward are as wild as the others. The wild stallions are the guardians of the bands. Always on sentinel duty, they give the alarm when the enemy approaches. In a moment the stragglers are rounded in, and a fleet-footed stallion leads the band and with the others at his flanks, away they go in a thundering charge. Nobody has yet been to able to overtake them. Sometimes they are lassoed or shot, but such a thing as heading them off in a race is out of the question.

The range of the wild horses at present extends from Texas to the southern Dakota line. They are more numerous in northern Colorado, Wyoming; and western Nebraska than anywhere else on plains. On the Republican river, on Divide between the South Platte, and Lodge Pole and the North Platte and far east as the heads of the Loup and Dismal rivers, the horses range at will. Five or six years ago they could be found on the divide between Sidney and Sterling in bunches of fifty or seventy-five, but now a bunch of twenty-five is considered large. Sometimes there is more than one in a band, but one of them is always acknowledged as chief, winning this distinction by many hard-fought battles with rivals. One bunch of eleven horses recently seen near Sidney was entirely composed of stallions; but this is explained on theory they were probably driven out of various herds when young, and gradually herded together, as old buffalo bulls are the habit of doing. From the horse ranch of M. E. Post, about fifteen miles north of Cheyenne, nearly 200 mares have wandered away, and it is believed that at least half of them have joined the wild horses.

The wild horses are compact little animals, weighing from 800 to 1,100. The majority of them stand about forteen hands high. In color, they are usually brown, sorrel, or bay. A gray is seldom seen unless it is a horse that has broken away from civilization. Their tails grow long, frequently dragging the ground, their manes are like those of other horses-and not flowing to the knees, as they are represented in some books. The eye, probably from being constantly on the watch is larger than the eye of the domestic horse, and even when tamed the eye remains a distinctive mark of the horse's origin. Wild horses, when captured and trained, are superior to any other the same size. Many of them are used by the cowboys, and others are broken for harness and driven as carriage horses, entirely trustworthy.

Several men living in Sidney make a living by catching wild horses. Until or six years ago no one knew how and very few outsiders now understand the methods adopted. Mr. Livingston of town describes the process as follows: "Two men always work together. Let them start out from Sidney, either north or south, and they are almost certain to find a bunch within fifteen miles. The plan is then to pitch a tent and camp, and one of the men, mounted on his best horse, carrying with him a few biscuits or something else convenient to eat, starts after the bunch. He does ride very fast, and at first does not attempt to get near them, but is content to keep the bunch moving, not allowing them stop and eat. The horses may go only a dozen miles, or they may go sixty; but, no matter how far they will turn back and seek the range which they started. If they go far, the mettle of the rider and his horse is tried to the utmost. The bunch must be kept moving, and there is no chance to change saddle horses until they turn, their own accord, and pass near the camp. Day and night, on they go. If the weather is clear and the nights not stormy, a rider will continue close after the sometimes half a mile off and sometimes within a hundred yards. It makes no difference whether it is dark or light, the horse that is ridden and trained follows after the herd. When the first rider succeeds in turning the bunch bringing them back to the camp, he is relieved by the second, who, with a fresh horse, starts after them, while his companion turns in and takes a much-needed rest. This time they will not probably go far. After a while they become tamer, and hunter can turn them at pleasure. This may require a week or it may be a couple of days. If the horses do not become scared they will not run far and are more easily managed. When the bunch becomes worried and starved out, it is driven toward the nearest corral. Formerly corrals were erected especially for the purpose, but new ranches are so numerous that they are not needed any more. Once inside, the wildest of the band are caught and chains fastened to their legs. Men walk among them and treat them kindly and they soon learn that there is nothing to be feared. They are turned loose into any ordinary pasture, and when they are wanted they are driven to the corral and roped. If two men can gather a bunch of ten; or a dozen horses in a week they of course make a good sum of money on the transaction as the animals will sell from $30 to $60 each; but misfortune sometimes overtakes them when in pursuit. The present movement of the stock raisers threatens to put a stop to the business. Mounted upon their grain-fed horses the hunters will pursue the wild bands when they are somewhat weakened by the winter. Riding as close as possible men will shoot the stallions from time to time. It is hoped that by spring nearly all the stallions will have been killed and that the capture of the mares will then be made possible.

*Cimarron New West* **(Cimarron, Kansas) 6 Jun 1885.** — The following are some of the telegrams received by a cattleman in Denver from a cowboy out on his range:

Hired three rustlers from Tin Cup at $25 and grub. Send arms and ammunition.

Had a seventeen-mile chase after the four Texans. Run down one horse, and got Jim laid up with a sprained ankle. Send down some grease and whiskey, particularly whiskey, sure. Don't forget whiskey four quarts. Get whiskey at Jones'. He has the best for medicine. If he has a three gallon cask better send that. Am a little sick myself.

Boss has been gone two days now, and nobody ain't seen him. Do you want me for boss?

Boss lit out with a young wider from Trinidad, and things all going to the dogs here.

## HANDLING THE LARIAT.
### Wyoming Letter to Philadelphia Times.

**The** *Tennessean* **(Nashville, Tennessee) 22 Jun 1885.** — I noticed a variety of lariats with a round-up party, nearly all of which were made of the very best quality of hemp, twisted so extremely tight that it was almost impossible to untwist the strands. Others are made of sinew cords, and were braided neatly, the ends or lassoing parts being greased so as to slip easily. Their lassoes were about sixty or sixty-five feet long, one-third of which forms the noose, and when swinging it is grasped a little above the loop, so as to prevent the same from slipping until launched through the air. The lasso is swung over the head and left shoulder and back over the right shoulder, a peculiar turn of the wrist as it begins to return, keeping the loop wide open. When flying through the air the noose takes a slightly oval form, keeping the loop wide open. But remains open and settles quietly around the object aimed at. McGaigan exhibited to me the modus operandi of handling the rope, and some of his feats performed in my presence were not only executed with marvelous precision, but were also beautiful to look at. This model cowboy is certainly an expert in his profession, perhaps the best rider and lassoist in the whole Northwest. What Slosson is to billiards McGalgan is to his profession.

One afternoon, while loafing around the campfire on the Musselshell, McGaigan and I got to talking about the skill he had acquired in throwing cattle and I had little difficulty in persuading him to let me into the secrets of his wonderful dexterity and actually showing me some of the finer points of the business. Mounting our bronchos we rode off through the sagebrush and out on the open prairie where numberless cattle were peacefully munching the luxuriant buffalo grass. My friend had his beat lariat fastened to the pommel of the saddle, and first showed me many fancy shots, throwing the lasso from or to any point, over either shoulder, behind or in front. He caught a tremendous bull by the horns, who looked up in surprise and started off like a steam engine, but the pony rode by the cowboy planted his forefeet firmly in the ground and checked Mr. Bull in his mad career before the latter got well started. The enraged steer went round and round in a circle at a 2:40 gait, the pony acting as a perfect pivot and turning slowly around with him, but it was no use: the bull was a prisoner and would have remained so had not McGaigan taken pity on him, and passed the wonderful ring down the line, upon which the rope leaped from around the horns and fell to the ground.

McGaigan remarked that it was no credit to catch a bull by the horns, for he cannot be thrown by them, and is simply held as a prisoner, but the skill in throwing a lasso is to pitch the noose just in front of an animal when he is going at full gallop, so that the next step he treads into it. He tried it on another bull while both of our ponies were jumping along on a dead run. The old fellow was going about as fast as we were, but the fatal loop shot through the air at a tangent and fell wide open, just in front of him on the ground. The left forefoot plunged square into the circle, the rope was tightened with a sudden jerk and the steer rolled over in the dust, as cleverly caught as anything I ever saw. The broncho too understood his part of the business thoroughly, for he bore at the right moment in the opposite direction, else he might have been thrown instead of the bull to which he was much inferior in weight.

McGaigan also caught great big steers galloping past at an angle by any leg. Not once was his judgment at fault. The noose whizzing through the air in every direction went as true to the mark as a bullet shot from a rifle.

I was much taken with the free-and-easy sort of life experienced by this roundup party and enjoyed my trip and camping out experienced so hugely that I was almost tempted to give up the profession of a scribe and a cowboy, but I thought better of it, next day and, although I had lots of fun and enjoyment, I concluded that cowboy life must have its dark as well as its bright sunny side.

> North Wyoming cowboys are kicking because they are now turned out to live on sage brush after sitting in the saddle seven months for barely enough to pay their board through the winter.

The *Billings Gazette* (Billings, Montana) 24 Nov 1885.

# Chapter 7: 1886

*"I tell you the cowboy is the happiest man in the world. No one to care for but himself, and he has his fun and spends his money, and when he is broke he hits the road for a job; as happy then as if he had his pockets full."*

-Letter from Montana, 1886.

## THE COLORADO COWBOYS.
### BY T. H. HITCHCOCK.

The *Poultney Journal* (Poultney, Vermont) 8 Jan 1886. — About 9 a. m. two cowboys and myself started for Byers where the "home ranch" is located. Ahead of us we drove our horses we were to ride in addition to the ones we were then using. The severe work of carrying a heavy saddle and rider up hill and down, all day long, is so hard on horses that each rider is furnished with several, which he rides alternately, or selects which he chooses, according to the work he expects to do. After having almost reached Byers, we met a messenger who told us to go to "East Gulch;" so we turned off at right angles and "loped" (eastern people call it canter or galop) across country, and arrived at East Gulch after about 25 miles' ride, just in time for dinner.

During our ride we saw several antelopes, three coyotes and great many rabbits, both jacks and cottontails, and I had the pleasure of killing a rattlesnake with my "quirt," a short, braided, pliable rawhide whip, used by cowboys and heavily loaded at its butt.

At East Gulch we found that the party I left in the morning had just arrived we also found the mess wagon, cook and eight cow boys, who had been hunting that part of the country for beef cattle, and who had just arrived with 375 head of four-year-old beef steers.

### HOW THEY "CUT OUT" CATTLE.

Let me tell you how well the cowboys understand their business and their horses. They had 375 head of cattle, and only wanted to ship 352, or 10 car loads of 23 head to a car. Therefore they wanted to "cut out" 23 head, which they proceeded to do as follows: All the cowboys rode quietly around the herd, and in that way got them closely bunched together, and almost perfectly quiet. Another cowboy, mounted on a reliable and well-trained horse, rode quietly into the herd, and by looking around soon saw a steer which was either too small or too poor to send with this lot. Gradually the cowboy works his way through the herd until he gets just behind the steer he wants to "cut out;" then the fun begins. In a moment the steer realizes that he is wanted, and turns to get away. A slight motion of the cowboy's hand wheels his horse back and forth and round on his hind feet, so that at every move the steer finds himself closely pressed by the horse and rider, and gradually pressed to the outside of the herd, until the riders on the outside see a chance to get behind him, and he is driven away from the herd. This process is repeated until all the cattle are cut out" that are wanted, and then the two droves are driven where and as these are wanted. Sometimes the rider is obliged to chase the steer on a run, back and forth and in and out among the drove before he can get him on the outside. While the rider is "cutting out," the rest of the cowboys are riding quietly on the outside of the herd and keeping them well bunched. This process is called cutting out, because the cattle find that each time they turn to get away, the rider has wheeled his horse in an opposite direction and completely cut off their escape. After the 23 steers had been cut out, the others were driven into the pasture and left until morning. This pasture is entirely fenced in, and is 43 miles around the fence, containing a tract of land almost 11 miles square, or over 100 square miles of pasturage, and ranges in altitude from over 800 feet higher than Denver to about 100 feet lower.

## THE LASSO ON THE PLAINS.

After the herd were driven to the pasture, two of the cowboys showed us how they "rope" cattle. They both started off on the run after a steer, and in a moment he became frightened and began to run to get away. Then the music began in earnest. The horses were urged to their fastest run, and as they slowly gained on the steer, each man began to whirl his rope around his head, keeping the noose open, and as soon as they were near enough the rope went circling through the air and settled squarely over the horns of the steer. The instant the noose was thrown in the air the rider wound the horn or pommel of the saddle, and the instant it settled over the steer's horns the horse stopped and braced himself firmly, and when the rope reached its entire length and tightened up, the steer was twisted around and stopped so sudden as to almost, daze him. In an instant he showed fight, and with head down started for the horse and rider who held him. When almost up to them the horse jumped to one side, and before the steer could renew his attack the other cowboy had thrown his rope around the hind feet of the steer and both ropes were tightened and the steer was thrown on the ground entirely helpless. The rope on his hind feet was held tight while the one on his horns was taken off and the rider had regained his saddle, then the other rope was loosened, and the steer, in trying to get up, of course kicked himself free. He was by this time thoroughly mad, and after standing a moment as if contemplating a fight, he finally started off on a trot and was soon far out on the prairie, free until again wanted. The behavior and training of the horses during the chase and roping was truly remarkable, and they showed a knowledge of just what to do, hardly excelled by their riders.

After this, the boys picked up pistols, stones, etc., from the ground while their horses were on the run jumped off and on the horses while in rapid motion, shot at a rabbit, also a target, with their horses on the run, killing the rabbit and hitting the bull's eye. Many other remarkable feats were performed which can only be accomplished after long and patient practice.

## SUPPER WITH THE COWBOYS.

About 4 p. m. the party I started out with left for Deer Trail, the point on the Kansas Pacific railroad from which the cattle were to be shipped for the following day, and I was left in a cow boy's camp. supper was soon ready; it consisted of warm biscuit, fried bacon, boiled ham, potatoes both boiled and fried, pickles, coffee as black as ink and drank with plenty of brown sugar, but no milk. We sat on the ground or reclined on the rolls of bedding and tents, and drank coffee out of tin cups. and ate off of tin plates with tin spoons and iron knives and forks; but I tell you the supper tasted good, and was eaten with lots of fun and jokes "on the side." After supper the beds were spread on the ground, and by 8 o'clock all was quiet except the crackling of the fire, the occasional bellow of cattle in the pasture, or howl from some angry or disappointed coyote, and the gentle patter of the light rain which fell from about 8:30 till 10 p. m. I was permitted to sleep in a little tent with the foreman, and I slept "like a log."

## SUNDAY LIKE OTHER DAYS.

On Sunday morning when I opened my eyes the boys had got the horses into the corral, had been out to see what part of the pasture the cattle were in, and had returned, bringing three "jack rabbits," which we had for breakfast. They also brought into camp four rattlesnakes which they had killed, one of which was almost six feet long with 13 rattles on his tail. Inside of him was quite a fair-sized "cottontail" rabbit, which he must have just swallowed. By 8 a. m. we had eaten breakfast and were in the saddle ready to start with the cattle for Deer Trail, which is about 15 miles from the camp. I drove the large herd of horses across the pasture, while the cowboys circled in the cattle and got them bunched and started out the gate in a drove. It is truly surprising how a few men on horseback can drive a large herd of cattle across a trackless prairie, over hills, across gulches and valleys, aud have them walk along as quietly and in the right direction as though they were old cows on their way to the well known barnyard for the evening milking.

About 1 p. m. we stopped in a gulch, where we found the cook with the mess wagon, he having passed us and reached this camping spot in time to have dinner ready for us when we arrived. The cattle were permitted to graze and drink while we ate our dinner, after which the foreman and myself rode ahead of the drove and arrived at Deer Trail fully two hours ahead of the cattle. We rode all around within a radius of five miles of Deer Trail, looking for three steers which had been injured by cars a few days previous; we could not find them, so rode back in time to help load the cattle when they arrived. Deer Trail is simply a shipping station for cattle, on the Kansas division of the Union Pacific railroad, about 50 miles east of Denver. Like Byers, it is the center of large cattle districts, and it has a population of only 60 or 70 inhabitants, but owing to the location it is the rendezvous for cowboys and cattle growers from all around that section. It supports a saloon with three billiard and pool tables, and quite good-sized boarding house, which is called the hotel. The words church, Sabbath and prayer-meeting are almost unknown, as Sunday is just like any other day in all such towns. Late in the afternoon the cattle reached the shipping pens and were quickly loaded into the train which stood in waiting, having been sent from Denver in response to a telegram from the station agent. The evening was spent by most of the boys in hanging around the saloon or store, while a few went to the camp early to bed, tired after a hard day's work: for it is a fact that driving a herd of cattle is to the cowboy about the hardest work he can do, for he is compelled to walk his horse all the time, and he cannot rest himself by getting off and walking awhile, for if a drove of cattle see a man walking they will stampede immediately; they will also stampede and become entirely unmanageable if they see a rider with a white shirt on, unless it is covered by a coat.

## THE PRAIRIE GRASS NUTRITIOUS.

To anyone from the east, the appearance of the grass on the prairie would lead him to think that a hundred square miles of it wouldn't be enough for a two-year-old steer to get a good meal from. This grass grows scarcely two inches high, and it is seldom seen even that high. It is curly and looks perfectly dry and dead, but if a careful observer will only pull up a tuft of it he will see that it looks healthy and has a rich sweet taste. It certainly is wonderful food for stock; the sheep all grow well, and their wool is soft and thick; the horses look plump and in good condition, notwithstanding the hard work they have to do; while the cattle are almost a marvel, for I never saw a lot of eastern corn-fed steers fatted for market by our thrifty eastern farmer that looked in any better condition than this lot of cattle did which have never tasted grain, and which in winter often have to paw away the snow to get this little, short, good-for-nothing looking grass on which they thrive and grow so fat.

## THE KIND-HEARTED COWBOYS.

During my trip I ate off a mess wagon, from tin plates, etc., and ate coarse, plain, healthy food, and slept on the ground in a small tent, and rode horseback from 25 to 75 miles per day, and I came home feeling stronger and considerably improved in health, with nothing but the pleasantest remembrances of a trip which to me was both novel and instructive. Right here, I want to correct an idea which is quite common in the East. The Colorado cowboy of today leads a laborious, rough and trying life, but he is not the ruffian and rowdy so often described by sensational reports and papers. I was never treated any more kindly or with any more consideration than I was during this trip. They did all in their power to make my visit comfortable and enjoyable, and thanks to their kindness, it was one of the pleasantest trips I ever made. They lead a rough and exposed life, they wear rough clothes and are always ready to handle anyone rough who deserves it, but they are an honorable, kind hearted and generous set of men, and I, for one, respect and like them. I saw several hundred cowboys during my trip, and I found them all to be rough, jolly, good-hearted fellows. I had such a good time that I shall very likely spend next spring and summer following the life of a cowboy, for I am convinced that this life is far superior to anything else in the world for gaining strength, health and restoration in to weak and diseased lungs, and for that reason I anticipate trying it for much longer next summer. — *The Homestead.*

## Letter from a Cowboy.

**The *Billings Gazette* (Billings, Montana) 25 May 1886.** — Editor Gazette: The roundup started to-day and the boys got together and appeared like so many bears that had been holed up all winter. We started out in the morning for the first roundup; some of the old cow horses did not like the idea of commencing for the summer and they would hump themselves and some of the boys were trying to bore post holes with their nose, and some took a notion to fly. It was fun for one like myself, but if I had been compelled to have taken the place of one of them it might not have been so funny. The stock men say they expect to brand more calves this year than ever before on the range, they branded more at the Musselshell crossing than they ever did at one time before Hanlon & Co. reaped a harvest from the boys but none of them got bad; some were feeling pretty well; some rode into the store to give their horses a glass of beer, but it was all in fun. I tell you the cowboy is the happiest man in the world. No one to care for but himself, and he has his fun and spends his money, and when he is broke he hits the road for a job; as happy then as if he had his pockets full. You will find some bad men among them as you will in every other class, but as a rule they are the most generous and free hearted boys that live, willing at all times to divide their last dollar with a friend. He likes the good things of this world and nothing is too high for him, no horse too good for him to ride, nor anything too good for him to eat, and then when he has married and settled down, if you go to his house you will find a neat little home and himself and wife as happy as can be. The roundup left this morning for the head of Haw Creek.

**BILL PONY.**
**Musselshell, May 22, 1886.**

## A SAD EXPERIENCE.

### How a Tenderfoot Is Broken into the Ways of the Wyoming Cowboys.

The *Daily Republican* **(Anthony, Kansas) 2 Aug 1886.** — A tenderfoot, or green hand, is not very cordially received by the cowboys, writes a Cheyenne, Wyoming correspondent of The San Francisco Chronicle. Wages are much lower than they used to be, and the riders blame the numerous recruits for the depreciation. Many of the newcomers quit the business after the first season, distrusted with their hardships, so that although there is a plentiful supply of apprentices, they never develop into plenty of good hands, and the experienced riders in an outfit have to do more than their share of the work. The most unpopular specimen of tenderfoot is the youngster whose father sends him out to the range to spend a college vacation or break extravagant habits. These "New York dudes," as they are indiscriminately called, are always sons of English stockowners friends, and they are prone, especially if fresh from college, to think very contemptuously of an illiterate puncher. If they let such a sentiment manifest itself the puncher promptly displays his sense of equality, if not, indeed, of superiority, and is quite ready to try conclusions on the spot. He dearly loves to guy a conceited youth, and does it very thoroughly when he sets about it.

"So you're from college, are you, Johnnie? We had a college buck in the 'Two Bar G" last year. Told us his old man was going to give him a big herd of his own, and gave every waddy in the outfit a song and dance about hiring him for his boss. When the round-up was camped nigh town he borrowed one buck's $30 spurs and another buck's $100 bridle, because he wanted to have his picture taken with a pony. Then he went back to college. You're pretty lean, ain't you, Johnnie? I reckon it ain't polite to call you Johnnie. Let's call him Fatty he'll fill up to it when he gits some old perslick bacon and beans into him. Can you ride, Fatty?"

Perhaps the bony youth rather fancies himself as a horseman and says: "I have been riding ever since I was 10 years old. I haven't tried my saddle yet, and I never rode anything but an English tree. But I was out with the Newport last season, and did pretty well. I guess I can ride these ponies anyhow. You talk about their bucking and all that, but I don't believe they are as hard to sit as a wicked three-quarter-bred horse." We ain't got any three-quarter horses, but we got some little ponies that's all-fired hard to stay with. We're goin' to clean out the strays in the bull pasture this morning, and that'll be a chance for you. Jim, you let Fatty ride that gotch-eared buckskin of yours. The boss won't mind, and Fatty ought to have a good horse to begin with. He's a little mean to saddle, Fatty, and he's kind of stiff-gaited in his lope sometimes, like as if he was pitching, but he's lightning after a cow."

When they go down to the corral someone obligingly ropes the buckskin, and, handing him over to Fatty, tells the latter to saddle up. The confusion of straps and the absence of buckles puzzle Fatty, and the boys, eager to see the fun, help him to saddle, the buckskin kicking and plunging all the while. When everything is in order Fatty prepares to mount. Just then the buckskin rears and falls backward. As he picks himself up again and stands lowering at Fatty, someone says: "If he goes to do that when you're on him tell him you're from college and he won't fall on you, young feller."

This time Fatty gets his hands on the horn of the saddle, and just as he is going to swing himself up the buckskin whirls and kicks his hat off. A kindly hope is expressed that his head is on loose, so that if the buckskin kicks that off next time it won't wrench, and then the boss tells Fatty to hold the check-piece of the bridle with his left hand until his leg is over the saddle, to prevent the horse's whirling: round again. He succeeds in mounting, and the prophecy that he will get off easier than he got on is no sooner made than it is fulfilled. Someone catches the buckskin, and the tenderfoot eagerly explains that he was not fairly seated before trouble began.

"We'll hold him for you, Fatty," and two stalwart waddies hold the buckskin by the ears until Fatty has screwed himself down in the saddle and clinched his teeth.

The buckskin walks off peaceably, and Fatty tries to feel at home in the round-seated saddle, longing for the knee-pads of the familiar English pigskin. He touches the buckskin with the spur to wake him up, and finds himself shot up in the air. He comes down on the horn of the saddle. Next trip up he lands on the buckskin's neck. The third ascension leaves him in the mud of the corral, with a corner kicked off his ear and every bone in his body jarred.

> The lasso artist among the Wyoming cowboys prides himself on hurling the noose in front of the beast so that he will step into it, entangle himself, and get thrown.

*Baxter Springs News* **(Baxter Springs, Kansas) 11 Sep 1886.**

> Charles Miller, a Wyoming cowboy, was killed in a drunken row in Lusk a few days ago.

**The** *Record-Union* **(Sacramento, California) 14 Oct 1886.**

# Tragedy of the Plains.
## Cheyenne Letter in New York Mail.

*Chicago Tribune* (Chicago, Illinois) 11 Sep 1886.

*New Ulm Review* (New Ulm, Minnesota) 29 Sep 1886.

*Jamestown Weekly Alert* (Jamestown, Dakota) 14 Oct 1886.

*Mullinville Mallet* (Mullinville, Kansas) 29 Oct 1886. — Cheyenne: a few days ago an old friend, last seen on the southern cattle trail. Old times were talked over. Our friend still followed the Texas longhorns, and many scenes of past days were recalled and many trail adventures recounted. In the course of the talk Red River crossing was mentioned, and our friend said he must tell of a romantic tragedy marking the crossing of the stream by the herd he was with this season. In the outfit, starting to gather the cattle for the trail in the early spring, was a young fellow about whom hung a mystery. He had been with the outfit since the fall before, and such was his reserve that six months had not succeeded in making him any better known to his companions than when he joined them. He was slight and delicate, in appearance to girlishness, yet his duty was always performed as well as that of the most stalwart rider. In the spring, when the activity of the cattle gathering began, this young fellow, to whom the boys had given the sobriquet of "Lady," became restless. An eager anxiety to see every stranger encountered on the range seemed to have taken complete possession of him. He seemed to know by intuition when a stranger was about, and was certain, sooner or later to get a sight of him.

"Lady" carried a good Winchester habitually, and knew exactly how to use it. It soon became a recognized fact in the outfit that the young fellow was looking for someone and the wild cowboys watched eagerly for the denouement. It did not come until the herd had been gathered and reached the Red River crossing. The night the outfit camped on the banks of the red stream there rode into camp a stranger looking for work. He was a stalwart, sun-burnt fellow, apparently about thirty years of age. As the foreman arose from his supper to meet the newcomer there came the rapid beat of hoofs. A horse dashed up to the group around the supper fire, a girlish form leaped to the ground, the firelight shone on the barrel of a leveled Winchester as it covered the stranger, and a voice, clear and stern, was heard: "Make your peace with your God at once, James Saunders. It is I, Ella Morrow, who speaks to you." A spellbound silence endured for a second's space and then the report rang out and James Saunders pitched headlong from his horse, shot through the heart by "Lady," the woman he had deserted. Scarcely had the smoke-wreaths floated upward when another report came and "Lady" had taken her own life. On the person of the girl, who had so long braved the hard life of the cattle frontier for the purpose of taking vengeance on her false lover, was found a letter. This told in pathetic terms the story of her wrongs. Up to her 17th birthday, three years from the date of the tragedy, she had lived a happy and beloved daughter, amid the granite hills of New Hampshire. On the 17th birthday there came a young stranger to her home. He was handsome, accomplished, and winning. Teaching the winter term of the district school, Ella was one of his pupils, and the close companionship in which they were thrown developed love on her part. It was the old story. Then came desertion and the secret departure of the girl from her home to avenge her wrongs. She had traced her betrayer to the Texas frontier, and knew that if she only had the patience to wait long enough she must meet him. Her task completed, she no longer had any desire to live. Reverently the rough riders, who had so long known her as a comrade, dug for "Lady" a deep grave on the spot witnessing her vengeance and laid her therein. The body of the seducer was carelessly flung in a shallow hole, and the next morning two lonely graves were left on the banks of Red River.

# Chapter 8: 1887

*"My horse's head, neck, and even their outlines were perfectly visible. I could not account for the phenomenal appearance of these lights. Afterwards, I learned that this thing sometimes occurs on the darkest nights during a rain and is caused by electricity. They were only visible for a few minutes, when they disappeared as mysteriously as they came."*

-Letter from Wyoming to Vermont, 1887.

A Rock Springs, Wyo., letter in the Cheyenne *Sun* says; "A few gentlemen from the range enjoyed their Christmas by riding around through the saloons, attempting to make their horses play the organ, drink over the bar, and play billiards, but aside from that the day was quiet."

*Chicago Tribune* (Chicago, Illinois) 16 Jan 1887.

# A STAMPEDE OF CATTLE.

## DANGERS OF GUARDING LARGE HERDS ON WESTERN RANGES.

### Handling a Herd at Night—Alarmed by Thunder—A Thousand Steers in a Mad Gallop.

A letter from Wyoming Territory to the New York *Herald* describes a stampede of cattle at night. The writer says:

The *Brandon Union* (Brandon, Vermont) 25 Feb 1887. — As possibly some may be ignorant of the manner of handling the beef herd at night, it may be well to explain right here. The "outfit" is divided up into "reliefs," usually two men to each, and each "relief" goes on herd in its turn and watches the cattle for two or three hours through the night. As night approaches several of the men ride out and "round up" the cattle as closely as possible without crowding them, on some comparatively smooth space not too far from camp. Alternately they are "rounded up" on the "bed ground" and have quieted down somewhat the first "relief" takes charge of them, and the two men ride slowly around the herd in opposite directions. If everything is satisfactory to his bovine majesty he will very soon lie down, and after chewing the cud of contentment or grass for a while doze off and snore as comfortably as men are sometimes said to do.

But to continue my story. A Mormon boy and myself were on first "relief." When we went to the herd, it had been rounded up and a few of them were already lying down. The majority of them, however, were grazing as eagerly as though instead of doing nothing but eat all the afternoon they had been fasting for a day or two. Every now and then some excitable "critter" would raise his head and sniff the air as if to discover the cause of his uneasiness, for cattle are as much affected by the change of temperature as the thermometer. They seem to know by instinct that something unusual is about to occur, and will plainly indicate by their actions the approach of a storm. Presently the wind stopped blowing, and it was but a short time before we had the most of the cattle lying down. It was growing very dark, however, with heavy, laden clouds slowly gathering over us, and we knew that although the elements were so quiet they could not be trusted and we were anticipating most any emergency. Our comparative peace was of short duration, for it soon commenced to rain, fine, drizzling, cold and penetrating. The cattle didn't like it, and at frequent intervals would express their dissatisfaction by low bellowings, and it was but a few minutes before they were all on their feet and seemingly possessed with the most ravenous appetite. The cold and the rain made them restless and, they all wanted to graze out on all sides of the bunch at once. We had to keep our ponies on a trot to keep them within bounds. The darkness rapidly grew denser and we could see an immense black cloud settling down upon us like a huge blanket. As we were gradually enveloped within its folds it seemed as if we were stricken blind. It was utterly impossible to see a thing. It sounds almost incredible but nevertheless is true. Several times I passed my hand in front of my face and could not even distinguish an outline. Several times I lost the herd entirely and was only recalled to it by the cough of a steer or the low singing of my companion, and once I rode square into one of them that gave a surprised snort and shuffled off in the darkness. Then I noticed a bright little spark appear at the tip of each ear of my horse. This was the only thing I could see. My horse's head, neck, and even their outlines were perfectly visible. I could not account for the phenomenal appearance of these lights. Afterward, I learned that this thing sometimes occurs on the darkest nights during a rain and is caused by electricity. They were only visible for a few minutes when they disappeared as mysteriously as they came.

Meanwhile, we were puzzling ourselves how to keep the cattle from leaving us, when finally the wind rose again, and driving the clouds before it, our sight was in a measure restored to us. The cattle turned tail to the wind and rain and started to drift with it. After riding once around the herd and getting them together we stationed ourselves a few feet in advance of the lead, and as they would crowd up to us we moved a few feet further ahead, the leaders would hold back until crowded upon us by those behind, when we would again advance a little. In this manner we kept them from going off, and, although we would not compel them to face the storm made them stand

and take it. We were congratulating ourselves that we had lost no cattle so far, as we were still pretty sure we had not seen the end of it, when we heard a low rumbling peal of thunder, frequently repeated and preceded by a distant but spiteful flashes of lightning. The rain increased, the wind came in quick and angry gusts and the cattle were showing their restlessness by crowding and hooking each other, and taking excited sniffs of the air. We realized that things were rapidly approaching a climax, and that it wanted only one sudden flash and loud report to make the already excited animals break through the slender bounds that held them and rush headlong possibly to their own destruction. In such an emergency our only hope was to keep them headed away from the creek, for if they should break and start in that direction it would be impossible to check them before they had plunged over the bank and to certain death below. With this object in view we were keeping ourselves as much as possible between them and the point of danger when the anticipated event occurred. There came a most blinding flash, instantly followed by a clap of thunder although the heavens had fallen. All courage and restraint instantly left each animal, and before the sound had hardly died away, every one of them was in a mad gallop, with head and tail in the air. Now was the time for our ponies to show their mettle as all depended upon their speed and sure footedness. Leaning forward in the saddle, and plunging the spurs into their flanks, we dashed along over the sagebrush and dog holes, which appeared like mammoth caves as our quick little animals deftly cleared them. Uphill and down we were riding side by side with the frantic leaders of the herd. We are crowding them all we can, using our "quirts" on the sides of their heads in the endeavor to turn them. With our repeated blows and continued crowding; they gradually swerve from their course little by little. If the pony should now make a misstep, or if he should miscalculate some jump he makes, and lurch from the saddle, we would never know how it happened, or ride on another stampede. But he seemed to know as well just where to put his feet as if he had been over the ground and practiced it all beforehand. We are gradually turning them in a circle, and lessening its circumference until finally we have them parked closely together, still running, and looking like an immense mill wheel. Those in the centre are merely turning around in their tracks while those on the outside are still running. Now we commence to sing to them in a low, crooning tone, which gradually has the wonderful effect of quieting them down, until finally they have stopped running entirely. As we ride around and pass them, they will occasionally elevate their noses and sniff at us and appear to be reassured. After about another half hour we have them again "bedded down" just where we stopped them and some two or three miles from camp. They are resting almost as quietly as if nothing had disturbed them, and as our time is up the "monnor"[16] rides into camp to call the second "relief." Presently I hear the clatter of their horses' hoofs and the jingling of their spurs, and after "Hello!" all around and a few answered inquiries as to how we "made it." I ride slowly into camp.

---

[16] An old Welsh term for friend.

Our faithful little horses are pretty well used up, and after pulling off their saddles and bridles and "picketing" them and throwing off some of our own wet clothing, we "turn in" to sleep soundly until the cook calls "Roll out!" at about half-past three next morning.

## Cattle on the Plains
### THE TWO CHIEF DANGERS IN WINTER — HOW THE BUFFALOES WERE EXTERMINATED
[Red Buttes (Wyoming) Letter]

***Bangor Daily Whig and Courier*** **(Bangor, Maine) 11 Apr 1887.** — There are two principal dangers to which stock in this country is exposed to winter. During the terrible storms which raged here, the cattle, if caught in position "drift" before the wind, until they reach some shelter or lee, which will measurably protect them. The prairie is more or less cut up at frequent intervals, by ravines and watercourses deeply worn through the plain, and usually with vertical or very steep banks. The beds of such ravines are sometimes twenty or more feet below the general level of the country. In winter, when much snow falls, these ravines become traps for cattle. The early storms fill them up with snow so that their surfaces are level with the prairie, and they look like little patches of snow-covered ground. There is nothing to give the cattle a hint of what is hidden beneath. A man would not attempt to ride over these little patches of snow; a horse would be too intelligent to plunge into them, but cattle are stupid. A storm comes up, the wind rises, and soon the air is full of horizontally driven particles of ice, which is hopeless to attempt to face. Woe to the man who is obliged to travel over the prairie during one of these storms. He cannot see twenty feet in any direction; to breast the storm is impossible. He can only travel with the gale, or quartering from it. Sometimes he can trust the steady wind for his direction, but in a broken country even this guide often proves untrustworthy, for hills and bluffs cause eddies of wind, which first make him turn from his course and end by hopelessly confusing him. Unless he knows the country inch by inch, he is sure to lose his direction and wander hopelessly until he brings up against some known landmark, or exhausted by his exertions, feels the fatal weariness creeping over him. How often this occurs no one in the East realizes. Last autumn, during the severe weather of October and November, the cowboys out on the late beef roundup suffered severely. Even before the winter set in, according to the almanac, one range rider, lost in such a storm, was found dead west of here, and three others lost one or both feet by freezing.

Drifting before one of these storms comes a bunch of cattle, perhaps ten in number, perhaps five hundred. With heads held low they move steadily along, strung out after one another. Long moans come from the group, and sometimes the sharper cry of an impatient calf. Long streams of steaming breath shoot from their ice-laden muzzles down toward the ground. On they go over the dim gray plain. The little calves keep close to their mother's side. Occasionally a young, weak calf staggers, then falls and mother stops behind to die with it. The rest keep on, particles of snow cling to their hair, the wind cuts them, they cannot pause to feed, and the storm may continue for a week. As they approach one of those snow-filled ravines, the leader walks into the snow, pitches forward, and in an instant disappears out of sight. The second follows and the next and the next. If the bunch be a small one, all are engulfed in the soft treacherous snow. If it be large, the cattle keep falling in and walking over one another until at length a solid mass of dead and dying animals makes a causeway on which the last may cross, to continue their way. In Wyoming's mountains, God does not temper the wind to the shorn lamb nor to the wretched cattle. Just so, in olden times, the buffalo, driven by the Indians, used to follow one another to their death when they jumped off the cliffs into the "pounds" below. I have seen ravines where, in spring and summer, decaying carcasses and white bones of cattle lay piled up so high that they half-filled the gulch,

This is one way in which cattle die here. Sometimes, but very seldom, a storm comes up without wind, and damp snow falls to the depth of a foot or two. This, if followed by cold weather, means absolute extermination to all cattle in the area covered by the storm. Cattle as I have said before will not "rustle," will not hunt about for food, will not dig through the snow to get at the grass beneath. If the feed is not before their eyes they just stand still and starve to death. If we may believe the traditions of Indians and old-time hunters, it was such a storm as this that which exterminated the buffalo on the Laramie plains where one could judge from the bleached bones that still dot those tablelands where they were very abundant. It was many years ago that this great tragedy took place, just how long is not exactly certain, but my authority thinks the date about 1845. Old Jack Robinson a venerable pioneer, now dead, told me the story many years ago. He said that in this terrible winter there came on the Laramie plains a heavy fall snow without any wind and the prairie was covered to a depth of four or five feet. During the next day or two the weather was warm and the snow begin to melt. Then followed a period of intense cold. A hard crust formed, the buffalo could find nothing to eat and, they all starved to death. Since that time there have been none on the Laramie plains, except a straggler which may have wandered down from the Sweetwater country to the northwest or from the mountains about North Park to the south.

# A Colorado Cowboy Cowardly Murders Another Near Trinidad.

## A COWARDLY MURDER.

### One Cow Boy Kills Another Who Was Lying on a Saloon Floor Half Drunk.

TRINIDAD, Col., June 17.—Word was brought to this city last evening of a tragedy that occurred yesterday morning at Indianapolis, a new town 30 miles from Trinidad, in which young McCarthy, a cow boy, whose home is in the Trinchera, was killed and John Caun shot in the leg. The murder of young McCarthy was cold-blooded and cowardly. The victim was lying on the floor of a saloon considerably intoxicated when another cow boy, whose name has not yet been learned, came up and asked McCarthy to get up and go with him. The young man replied that he would and rolled over with his back to the speaker who, without another word, drew his revolver and shot McCarthy through the head killing him instantly.

*Star Tribune* (Minneapolis, Minnesota) 18 Jun 1887.

## DAKOTA COW-BOYS.

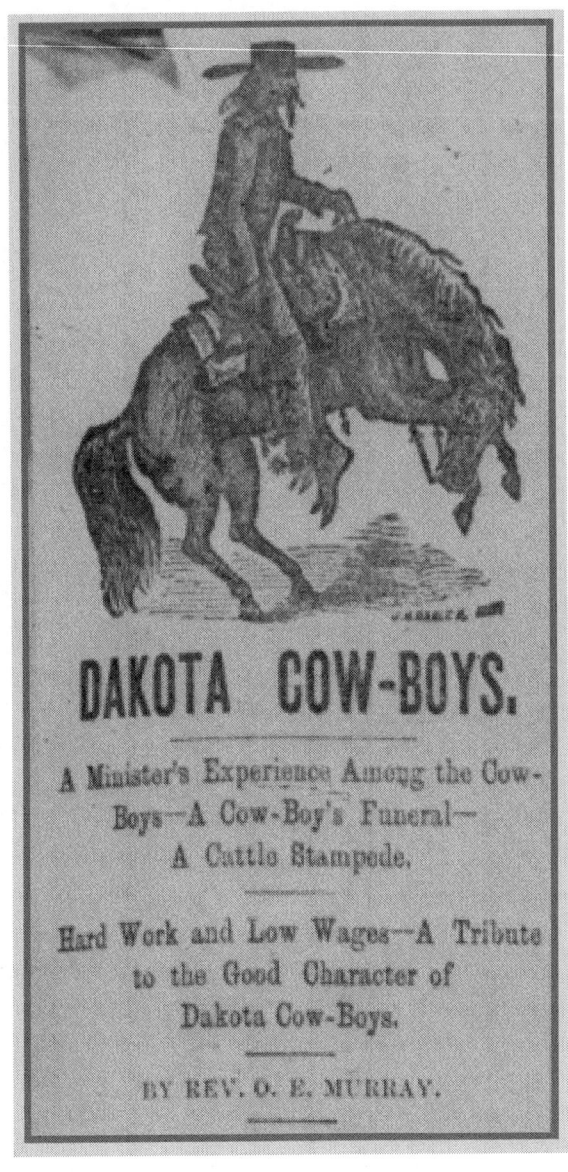

A Minister's Experience Among the Cow-Boys—A Cow-Boy's Funeral—A Cattle Stampede.

Hard Work and Low Wages—A Tribute to the Good Character of Dakota Cow-Boys.

BY REV. O. E. MURRAY.

*Spearfish Weekly Register* **(Spearfish, South Dakota) 1 Jul 1887.**
— Since my return to this side of the Missouri so many questions have been asked me concerning the Cow-boys, that I cheerfully accept your invitation to describe these much abused and

misrepresented men. To judge classes of men by the bad deeds of some individuals is not just and is very misleading. In this way our railroad men have been subjected to suspicion, and false estimates placed upon their general character because of a few reckless ones of the early days. The work of both railroader and cow-boy is rough and calls for nerve, but they should not be abused. Both classes are large-hearted, honest, daring men as far as I know them.

Great injustice has been done the cattlemen of the Northwest. Our Dakota cow-boy differs from his frolicksome brothers of Florida or Texas. These seem to be indigenous to the pine, palmetto and pampass region and doubtless have performed many of the feats for which they are se widely famed. A few of these have painted frontier hamlets red, stolen unbranded cattle, and have often killed their man, but it is unfair to think that all cow-boys do so. Those infamous police papers with their profane caricatures have done more to put false ideas into the east concerning the cow-boy than all other influences combined. The smallest deed is grossly exaggerated until it seems *monstrum horrendum,* yet most of the boys take these miserable, lust-ful sheets. A camp of Texan cowboys attempted a reform some years ago. It was agreed that the man who threw a gray-back on the floor, or combed his hair would be fined two bits— 25cts. Soon the camp had quite a little revenue from this source. It was proposed to order a newspaper, so those in the camp were ordered to write the name of the paper each preferred and put the ballots into a hat. But the majority could not write and were given *vive voce* privilege after the ballots were counted. The vole by ballot stood for leading political journals and was a little divided. The vote by acclamation was solid. All shouted as if in one voice. *P'lice News.* When asked the reason for their choice, thy replied: "We don't keer fer yer tony *Tribune* an *Posts*; we aint eddicted nuff to read em, fellers. We like *P'lice News* or Gazette kase we kin read the picters. D'ye catch on?"' This story is told by Sirigio. a genuine Texas cowboy. My experience with cattle men of Dakota furnishes no example of such ignorance though I am sorry to say that the same vile and venomous slush visits most of the dugouts, cabins and ranch homes of the west. What an opportunity - here for missionary effort. Send out your illustrated Christian paper and remind the boys of home and mother once more.

During all my stay with the boys at their camps, on the round up, and frequently ruffling them in town, they always treated me kindly. On one occasion they attempted to treat me a little too kindly. Just outside of a frontier saloon a number of the boys suddenly confronted me. The greeting was hearty but not all they desired. They insisted on my taking a drink with them. I was pulled into the saloon and made to stand before the bar. "What'l ye take?" said one to the other, and they took. It came my turn to "take" and I sang out "lemonade!" They seemed insulted and were bound to pour something stronger down my throat: But the bartender with a trusty "45" came to the rescue, saying, "a man has a right to call for his own drink over my bar," and I had as good a lemonade as ever I drank. These same cowboys would fight for me any time. Some years ago a minister came among the cow-boys and attempted to reform them by conforming to their ways. He drank, smoked and even played cards with them. Of course they had no respect for him and once got him so drunk that he died from effects of the liquor. The cow-boys hurried him in the Bad Lands a hundred miles from any settlement. His only funeral service was a volley of oaths and another from their guns over the sad end of the misguided man. Drinkers, whether cow-boys or no, have no respect for a minister that conforms to their ways and trims to catch their breeze.

My first interview with a cow-boy taught me a lesson on that line. Various stories, more or less colored, of my cow-boy funeral have floated through the eastern and western press. In some of these accounts I hardly know myself. The matter grew until I was pictured standing over the dead man holding two revolvers, preaching away. Now, I have never carried a revolver in my life and never owned one until one of my boys hearing that I was to preach in Sioux City on my return from the Hills, gave me his own gun remarking, "That's where they kill preachers ain't it? Waal' take this, pard, and ef they git arter yeou, pepper em." He made me take it and I have it yet. That funeral was about as near as I remember like this: We had just ended an afternoon service when a cow-boy king who had the reputation of killing a man or two, came up the broad centre aisle of my church. His wide brim sombrero hat was under his arm, spurs clinked at his heelsjnd in a rough voice he accosted mc with, "Be yeou the preacher?" I said "yes, sir." "Waal, I hearn tell you was," he drawled out. "Say, one of our fellers gin eout last night." "Yes," I said sick?" "Naw, wusser'n that, he kicked, that is he kicked the bucket. Jim was a tough cuss, but he's gone over the range. Say, the fellers wanted me to ax yer to come down 'n say somethin' over 'im. An' the boys wanted me to gi' yer some directions." "Yes," I said with the emphasis that says "go on." "Neow you must promise that you won't do ez some gospel sharps do, yank a man all over hell arter he's dead. Will yer mind." He fixed his keen eyes upon me and looked into my-eyes as he spoke. I replied, "If you want me to give Jim a decent Christian burial I will go with you, but I shall not 'promise' what I shall do, nor 'mind' what I shall say." "You won't he gasped. "Do you naw who yer talking to?" "I have not had the honor of your acquaintance I said. He reached out his big honest hand and as we shook heartily he said: "By gum! You'r just the feller az we like, you shall preach over Jim what you please. The best kerriege in this town ain't none too good for the likes of you. Soon the presiding elder and I were going to the funeral in the finest carriage in town. The sermon was held in a dark back room, quite a bit underground. It wasn't one of the most romantic surroundings for a funeral I ever witnessed. Chaplain J. McCabe was in the audience and often tells this story.

  The cow-boy is as much of a roamer as a Methodist preacher, and often among the parks and valleys of the Wyoming side of the Black Hills would I meet some of, the boys that remembered the famous funeral It fell to my lot to marry some of the same men and they treated me handsomely. One of them came over from Montana, across the corner of Wyoming and came up to the Hills, a distance of 150 miles. He would have me marry him and though I was twenty miles from home, he awaited my return. Such fees as these men gave I never met before.

At the agricultural fairs in the Hills they have roping contest. They give a wild steer a certain start, then the boy of the plains with his best pony takes after the steer, throws a lariet over his horns, throws him on his back once or twice and ties three feet into a hog hitch. It is a most exciting performance and the wilder the steer the better they throw. The champion thrower of all the cowboys is Mr. Jesse Driscoll, of Spearfish. I witnessed his best throw. He tied his steer after throwing him twice in 58 seconds from the time he took after him. Best time on record. A short time after this Jesse and his girl came to my parsonage and were married. One of the attendants said that I tied him faster than he did the steer and in about the same time. Jesse owns a large bunch of cattle and is succeeding grandly on the Little Missouri.

The time of cattle men is consumed in driving on the trail from the pastures to market, with the round-up and branding in between. The round-up is the dangerous and exciting time. The cattle scattered through gulches, canons and bail lands, are gathered together and each band put by themselves. The dangers arise from fierce steers goring man and beast, pony stepping into badger holes and breaking its leg or the neck of its rider. The boys are often thrown and it takes two to five days to get medical aid. The average life of a cow-boy is less than five years. Their pay $30 to $40, per month. Very meager remuneration for what they endure.

One of the liveliest sights I ever saw was a cattle stampede. We were between the Missouri and Cheyenne rivers. A storm was coming up and the animals, propelled by instinct, broke into a wild run. How they bellowed! Ears erect tails lashing, they were as unmanageable as a cyclone. If Longfellow had ever seen a stampede he would not have called them "dumb, driven cattle." These were driving all before them. Occasionally one would fall only to be tramped to death by a thousand hoofs. Their path was strewn with the carcasses thus slain. The cow-boys all rode on one side of the herd to make them circle as much as possible. A night stampede is most dangerous and destructive. The branding of calves and colts is a novel part of this work and would take more space than you can spare to describe fully. Only let me say it is no such tame affair as putting the U. S. on cavalry horses. When horses or cattle change hands, the brand must have a vent burned into the animal near the former owner's brand. It is equal to a bill of sale. To catch a wild unhandled horse the lariat is used. Best ropers catch the foot. How they fight for liberty. They never yield till exhausted. If caught around the neck they never drop until the wind is choked off. Then with blood running from both nostrils they fall to the ground. The feet are tied and the branding is soon done. It is cruel work at best and this is what makes western ponies so hard to handle. The memory of this cruelty makes them fidget and caper. They seem to be always expecting something to happen.

Women can often catch these horses when men can not. They seem to know that a woman never inflicts pain upon them. The settler is creeping upon the cattle king. They often have feuds similar to the quarrel between the herdsmen of Abraham and Lot. The cow-boy is bound to die out in time. Only a matter of one generation and the man that rides his broncho equipped with lariat, spurs and six shooter- with a braided whip called a "quirt" in his hand, dressed in a broad brim sombrero with a slicker either on or tied to his saddle, with finely laced leather "shacks" or trowsers, dashing recklessly over the treeless plains, will be no more. He will only exist in imagination and will be looked up on as Robin Hood and his bowman an extinct class.

Do not connect Hood's thieving the deeds of Texans, Mexicans, or Floridians to your picture of our cow-boy. The best boys ever - threw a lariat, roped a steer, branded a calf, shot an enemy or followed a grub cart, are found on the Bad Lands and plains of Dakota. Never were finer cavalry than these. A Sheridan or Logan would have been proud of them. Their generosity is proverbial. The hardest workers, most honest lot of men I have ever met are these caricatured, much lied about cow-boys. I long for another ride with them on the range, another bunk in the dug-out and the song and frolic of the camp-fire.

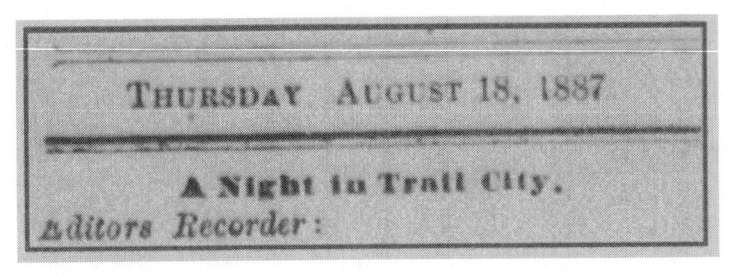

> THURSDAY AUGUST 18, 1887
>
> **A Night in Trail City.**
>
> Editors Recorder:

***Westmoreland Recorder*** **(Westmoreland, Kansas) 25 Aug 1887.** — Trail City is on the Arkansas river, in Colorado, only a mile from the Kansas line. In May, June, and July it is a lively place, at other seasons it is dull and quiet. I was through in April—the houses were empty and the town seemed deserted. A coyote had taken lodging in one of the buildings and snarled at me as I stood in the doorway. I could easily have killed the brute, but being the only living creature that I saw in the place, I suffered it to live.

I went back to the town in June and stayed overnight. I found everything changed. My former acquaintance, the coyote, was not to be seen and the house where he had resided was occupied as a saloon. Immense herds of cattle from Texas arriving every day and the place was full of cow boys, gamblers, girls of the demi monde class, greasers, blacklegs, etc., and a majority of these people were fuller than the town. There was no vacant houses, and huge tents were used for stores, hotels, dance houses, gambling booths and saloons. The place resembled Dodge City in her palmy days. Things were quiet enough during the day, but when evening came and the cow boys poured into town the fun commenced, if that can be called fun which has little in it that appeals to person who respects order or decency. On the streets were painted Jezebels who made their unnatural solicitations openly. The saddest sight on which human eyes have ever looked is a fallen woman, shameless in her degradation. As woman in her purity and innocence is the noblest and sweetest of all created things, when she has thrown her chastity away she is the vilest and most depraved. When we see such loathsome creatures and think that the stainless mothers and maidens of our land belong to the same race and sex, there rises in our hearts the feeling that prompts men to destroy. Nevertheless those who have been betrayed and led astray are to be pitied while they are abhorred, though pity cannot cleanse the slime of their pollution. O, the shameless creatures! What bitter blasphemy they utter oaths that would scorch the lips of innocence, and vile words, spoken as if they were the choicest gems of language. Is it possible that they were ever sweet-faced little girls that fathers kissed and mothers loved so tenderly, the light and and joy of happy homes? Is there a mother alive to-day, who, if she knew her infant daughter would grow up to this, would not strangle her in her childhood, if there was no other way to save? Better to see her die a thousand deaths, wasted by slow disease and tortured by fierce pain, enjoying agonies that cannot be conceived, than come to such a fate.

Bang! Whiz! Clatter, Clatter! tramp, tramp! "Whoop!" "Hurrah!" A dozen horsemen dash down the street at full gallop, shouting and shooting as they ride. They are only cow boys "painting the town." People on the street rush to cover, lights in the houses are instantly extinguished, there is noise of shivered glass where a window has been struck by a stray bullet the riders vanish in the night and the hoof beats die out in the distance. In five minutes the event seems to be forgotten; the saloons are again in full blast, the dance houses resound with the notes of squeaky fiddles and the tread of drunken feet that vainly attempt to keep time to the phthisicky music, and over the gambling tables is heard the chink of changing money. It is needless to describe these resorts. What Abilene was twenty years ago and Cheyenne, Wichita and Dodge City have each in their time been since, Trail City was when I visited it in June. The mining towns of the Rocky Mountains, though bad enough as a rule, are scarcely as reckless in their drunken revels.

It was late when I went to bed, nearly midnight, but no one else in the town appeared to have any thought of retiring. Twice in the night I was roused by the firing of revolvers and once there was a cry of "Murder!" Again towards morning I heard a woman's voice in the street declaring in tones loud enough to be heard all over town that she was a "she devil" and could drink blood. I have reasons to believe that she told the truth. I was glad when the sun rose, the same sun that shines on peaceful homes elsewhere, and was thankful that the class of towns of which Trail City was the prototype is passing swiftly away.

Recently, within the last month, the cattle trail has been abolished and the land opened for settlement. Already it is pretty nearly all taken either as homesteads, pre-emptions or tree claims. The business of driving cattle north from Texas is ended forever. Trail City will never be again what she was when I visited the place in June. No other town will take her place. It is better so civilization thereby wins an-other victory.

**SYLVESTER FOWLER.**

---

**COLORADO LETTER.**

Dude Cowboys and the Trappings They Wear—Selling Hats by Weight—A Cowboy's Superstition About Blue Bronchos and Red-Headed Women.

[Special Correspondence.]

---

The *Wilkes-Barre News* (Wilkes-Barre, Pennsylvania) 19 Oct 1887. — Aug. 15. This edge of Christendom is coming to be one of the leading cattle sections in the United Sates. It escapes the droughts that cause such loss in Texas, the terrible snows that decimate the herds of Montana, or the crowding of settlers that has broken up so many ranches on the plains of Colorado and Kansas. Here and there through the main range of the Rocky Mountains are such plateaus as the Uncompahgre Plateau, just above us here, ranging from fifty to one hundred and fifty miles in length and fifty to seventy-five wide. Covered with springs, they present a beautiful exception to the arid condition of the Rocky Mountain country, and pasturage is more than abundant. It is a common sight in riding over the plateau to see deer and cattle, intermingled, feeding in grass up to their backs. In the winter the herds drift down before the snows off of the high altitudes into the canyon pasture lands below, where the feed is abundant for grazing during the short winter. It is rare that the herdsman here has to keep his cattle in the low lands longer than eight weeks. Whether in the canyons or up in the high altitudes, the water is always plenty. Some of the most beautiful bubbling springs in the world are to be found upon the plateau. There is abundant shade also from the pinon belt on up through the magnificent yellow pine belt into the spruce parks that fill the highest part of the plateau.

Of course, now that the country is full of cattle, the cowboy is a common sight. A great many Eastern men have invested capital in cattle here, and, consequently, there are a good many nephews, sons and brothers-in-law of rich men doing service as cowboys. The old settlers call them dude cowboys. The outfit of an ordinary cowboy is a very simple affair, but a very serviceable one. Deerskin is plenty, and there are deerskin tailors who can make an excellent pair of leggings and hunting shirt with any amount of fringe and decorations on them, so that for ten or fifteen dollars the dude cowboy can dress very much as old Leatherstocking himself. The cowboy hat is to be had in any outfitting store. Stitson ships tons of them out here every year, although you never see them in the stores back East. When the cowboy wants a hat he goes into any outfitting store, and in a very quiet, shy way intimates to the clerk his want. The storekeeper reaches up to a shelf and dumps down on to the counter a dozen or fifteen hats. They are made of the best felt, nearly a quarter of an inch thick.

Some are white, some are drab; now and then there is a blue one, seldom a black one.

*SELLING HATS BY WEIGHT.*

The cowboy loves the white one, which, after a few months service, takes on, like a meerchaum[17] pipe, a delicate buff tint. Trying on one hat after another, he finally indicates his choice. The next action of the storekeeper would make an Eastern man open his eyes wide. In the most matter-of-fact way the clerk puts the hat on the

---

[17] A soft white claylike material consisting of hydrated magnesium silicate.

scales and weighs it, for he knows the cowboy hat is sold by weight, the price of the best quality of hats being a dollar an ounce. A real dude cowboy never wears a hat weighing less than ten ounces. Of course any amount of ornamentation may be put upon the hat. There are deerskin thongs and tassels and bead-worked cartridge belts to be worn around the crown, and usually kept two thirds full of cartridges.

No dude cowboy fails to wear a broad, stout belt, in which he keeps the best six-shooter dollars can buy. Most of the dudes practice pistol firing diligently and are good shots, but the old time cowboy long since abandoned his fire-arms and rides his horse with as little unnecessary baggage as possible. The dude cowboy is very fond of his feet, and he wears the best boots his money can buy. A high heel delights his eye, although it is an awkward thing to ride in and of no earthly use. Top boots are affected by most of the dude cowboys, and few of them ride without the Mexican saddle leggins, richly decorated with the figure of a mountain lion couchant.[18] They are a very good protection to the legs while riding through thickets and along rough, craggy mountain trails. Twenty-five dollars is the lowest that any cowboy pays for his saddle, and some squander a hundred on it. The saddle that costs the latter price is richly ornamented by hand and is very complete in its way. No cowboy ever wears an overcoat, and none ever goes without his slicker. The slicker is a strong linen coat reaching to the heels, soaked in boiled linseed oil. It is the most convenient garment a frontiersman can wear. Beneath him at night it

---

[18] Lying down especially with the head up.

makes a good bed, in a rain it is a complete protection; for his noonday lunch, strapped over two limbs, it makes a splendid awning. It will stand any amount of dirt and grease, and wear and tear. Rolled up and tied in his ladigos[19] it takes up very little room. Every cowboy must have at least three horses in the active part of the year. In the spring and fall "round ups," and while hunting after stray cattle late on in the fall and after part of the winter up in the higher altitudes he has a good deal of hard work to do. There is no fun about his life at those times.

The notion now is with the real smart cowboy that he wants a blue broncho. There is a sort of superstition about the color — that is to say that a blue broncho is a great many times tougher than a sorrel or a bay or a white. Tom Gallagher, an old-timer, who never can say good morning without swearing, but who is a prime good fellow from his heels to his scalp, has made a large fortune in colors. As Tom tells it: *"You see I kinder had known about this thing from the start. My wife had red hair, and she was a mighty smart woman 'round the house. She looked after all the cows, fed the pigs, kept the boys and girls straight and clean, never minded cooking the meals and then, upon a pinch, would saddle a horse and help me on the range. In those times that counted, for I hadn't more dollars than I could keep in my pocket, so I always bet on red-headed girls. When my first woman died I waited five years before I came across another red-*

---

[19] A long strap on a saddletree of a western saddle to adjust the cinch.

headed girl to marry. They was plenty yaller-headed and black-headed girls, but I wouldn't hev em.

Somehow or other, I got a pair of blue bronchos when I first came out into the valley. They did so well that I always bought blue bronchos after that.

I've got now about eight ponies, every derned one of them is a blue broncho. When I came to my cattle — and it was derned few I bought when I started — I had a chance to buy a black Galloway bull. I bought him on his name, not his color. I thought it would be a big thing to buy a bull after my own name. Wall, that black bull has turned all my herd black. I have sold every other cow I had in the first place until I haven't got anything but black critters, and the way these fellows do butt is a caution. I can put more beef on four legs with my black critters than any man between Denver and Salt Lake, and I tell you it makes money. It saves on freight the same set of legs can carry two or three hundred pounds more meat to market. So I tell all young fellows going into the cattle business to bet on red-headed gals, blue bronchos and black bulls. Those are the three that make the money." Whether these superstitions are correct or not, they have carried the day. Nobody buys an outfit in this section now without trying to follow Tom's advice, at least as far as the blue bronchos and the black bulls go. Red-headed girls are scarce.

**JOHN GALLOWAY.**

# THE COWBOYS.

## SOME STORIES CONCERNING THEIR LIFE OUT WEST.

### How They Made a Pompous Railroad Conductor Dance—Why They Take Charge of a Town Occasionally—Exaggerated Tales of Wild Deeds—Exquisite Horsemanship.

The *Kinsley Graphic* (Kinsley, Kansas) 4 Nov 1887.

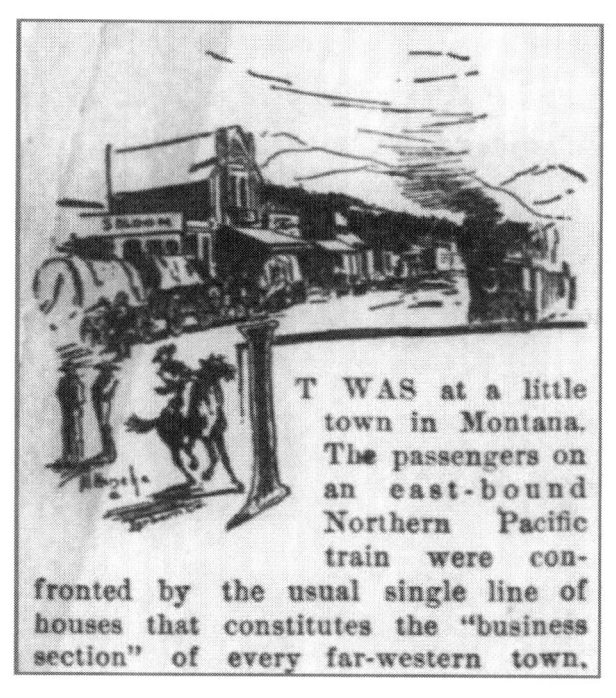

T WAS at a little town in Montana. The passengers on an east-bound Northern Pacific train were confronted by the usual single line of houses that constitutes the "business section" of every far-western town, but there were one or two brick houses in the block, which was a strange and welcome sight, and one of these bore on its face a sign in black-and-gold, announcing a "licensed gambling saloon." On the long, broad depot platform was something else that was unusual a loungers gathering of at least two-score young men. They were talking in little knots, leaning against the depot, staring at the passengers gossiping with the train hands, whistling, whittling, expectorating, and in all respects behaving precisely like the average railroad depot lounger wherever you see him, whether in New Jersey or New Mexico. They were cowboys. The word was passed among the passengers, and nearly all looked at them curiously. Could it be possible, was, I doubt not, the thought in the minds of every Eastern man or woman who looked at them. Had it been said that they were farm-hands on a holiday, or even idlers of the town, store clerks, carpenters, porters, or what not, no one would have wondered.

But cowboys! Why, there was not a pistol to be seen on the person of one of them. There was not a pair of fringed leggings in the crowd. There was not a leather jacket among them. They were a band of young fellows in rather coarse and not always well-fitting clothes, with sunburned faces, a tendency toward soft hats of rather wide brim just such men as we had been seeing ever since we left Portland, Ore., and the Pacific coast. There was one horse, the typical cayoose of the plains, hitched to the platform, and while the train waited a tall, finely-featured fellow with a jet black mustache and spurs on his small, neat boots called out to another, "Kin I take him?" and instantly flung himself on the little beast, clapped his heels against the pony's side and was off like the wind. Everybody looked, for it was a graceful and spirited bit of horsemanship, and all saw the rider and pony turn the far corner of the business buildings and disappear. In an incredibly short space of time the tattoo of the fleet little hoofs was heard again and the man had returned, leaped from the pony to the platform and was chatting with the others.

"Cowboys?" said the brakeman of the Pullman sleeper. "I guess you'd think they were if you had been right on this platform three months ago. We had a conductor who was a very pompous sort of a man, very haughty and apt to swell out his chest and walk around like a drum major when he thought any one was looking at him. Few men put on airs of that sort in this part of the country, and, though it was his nature and he could not help it, this way of his attracted a great deal of attention. One day the cowboys were here in full force. They had just finished their round-up, and had been drinking enough to make them feel first rate. They made up their minds to have some fun with this conductor that I speak of. Along came the train and he came with it, standing on the platform with one arm out ready for the grand tragedy actor's wave he always gave as he sang out the name of the place. But he never waved that time. His arm was grabbed and he was pulled into the middle of the ring the cowboys had formed.

"Now, come off your stilts and dance us a jig,' said the leader.

"'Really, gentlemen — '

"Bang, bang, went two revolvers. Every cow-puncher had taken out his gun and aimed it at the conductor's feet.

" 'Dance, or we will shoot the shoes off your feet,' said the leader. Bang, bang, bang went the revolvers again.

"Did he dance? You had better believe he did. He jigged and shuffled and flung his legs around like a well, not like a dancing master, for he had never done so undignified a thing as to dance before in his life, but rather like a calf stung by a million hornets. When the boys got tired they put up their pistols and walked away and he got off with his train. He was madder than a man who finds all the buttons off his shirt when he's dressing to catch a train; but, pshaw! they didn't mean nothing. The cowboys are the best people in the country.

And, in truth. If there is any force in iteration, and any strength in unanimity, we must believe that the cowboy's character has been much belied, for all the people who live in the cowboy country say the same thing. "They have been outrageously misrepresented in the

Eastern newspapers," said the Hon. Theodore Roosevelt, who is himself what is called a "cow-man" or ranch-owner, in talking of these people to me. "The cowboys are the natural police of the grazing country. Some of the truest, bravest, finest men in all that concerns manhood that I have ever seen are cowboys. The murders and deeds of violence ascribed to them are mainly the acts of bullies, gamblers, adventurers and lawless characters of all sorts who used to infest the plains but are being rapidly run out of the country by the cowboys."

But it is my purpose to tell in this letter what I heard told of the cowboys, giving it for what it is worth, and being impressed by the fact that all who spoke to me of these dashing cavalrymen of the ranges were their friends, and agreed with what Mr. Roosevelt further said that "sometimes when they come to a town after a long absence from civilization and with money they have been longing to spend, they occasionally drink a little too much, and become hilarious, but it is to be remembered that in most of the little settlements they meet with the only means of diversion are apt to be immoral, the liquor is bad and the society is in a primitive condition."

One man on the train who had lived among the cowboys many years recalled an incident in one of these invasions of a little town. It was in Dakota. One of the boys had noticed that in a certain saloon, whenever a customer called, the bartender put the palms of his hands on the bar, bent his elbows wide apart, leaned over and said in a most affected manner, "What will it be this time, sir?" The cowboy sense of humor seems to be keenly developed, and nothing excites it so quickly as an artificial or pretentious manner in a man. The cowboy who had observed this peculiarity in the bar tender awaited his chance and entered the saloon when no one else was in it. The bartender at once leaned over in his favorite attitude and asked "what it would be."

"Move an inch and you are a dead man," said the cowboy, instantly leveling his pistol at the bartender. "I like your pose and want to print a picture of you on the wall."

With that marvelous accuracy of marksmanship born of constant practice with pistols, which is one of the characteristics of these centaurs of the West, the cowboy began shooting with great rapidity, first with one revolver and then with another, and another, in such a way as to outline the entire upper half of the bartender's form with bullets that literally scraped the clothes of the victim. Whatever was in the way of the bullets was shattered, including a mirror, several bottles, a vase of flowers and I know not what all, but the bartender was not once scratched. The next day the same cowboy entered the same saloon and said: "Make out a bill for what damage I did. I was drunker'n a boiled owl when I mussed up your place yesterday."

In Victoria, I met with one of those Englishmen met with in all out-of-the-way places and with whom England peoples all the tracks of travel, who had been apparently everywhere in the world. He knew the Natal country as you know the pocket of your coat; he had lived in the Australian bush; he had dined with Kalakaua and roanfed the Rocky Mountains, and had his feet washed and a guest's nightgown brought to him by a young girl in Iceland, as is the custom there. One trip of his had been taken in consequence of reading of the wild life in the Black Hills country a few years ago, and after a time spent there he drifted through the range, or cowboy country. I will repeat to you some of the things he said he had noticed about the cowboys, and in his exact language, but I regret to say that I cannot hope to make it appear as it did to me, for his tone and manner and facial expressions were as peculiar as his words.

"The cowboys are a rum set of beg-gahs," said he; "as good a lot of rough-and-ready boys as you'll run across in the wide world. They are a little wild at times, you know, "but, bless you, they mean no harm. I got into a town one night and it was filled with these fellows all 'flush' as they call it when they've plenty of money a condition so unusual with them that they always hasten to spend every penny in order to feel natural again. They were riding up and down the street and shooting right and left like wild Indians in a battle. What they were shooting about I really can't say as I thought myself safer indoors than if I went out and ran into one of their bullets. The next day there was a poor clark[20] bending over a desk in one of the stores, don't you know, setting down his sales and saying not a word to anybody, when up rode a drunken cowboy on his pony, dashed into the store through the open doorway, whipped out his devilish revolver and shot the poor clark through the head. Now, to show you how the cowboys regard that sort of thing, you know, let me add that they hung that drunken chap almost as quickly as he had done for the poor clark.

---

[20] Clerk.

And there not being any trees handy about they made no bones of the want of them, but hung him from the roof of a railway carriage that happened to be standing there at the time.

"They're a very rum lot," he continued. "They are so enormously proud of their feet that they never buy shoes that will fit them. If a new pair of shoes can be got on a cowboy's feet with the combined strength of the clark and the proprietor and the cowboy himself he imagines they must be shockingly unfashionable in size. I was in a shoe store one day when two men had succeeded in getting the foot of a cowboy into the smallest man's shoe in the place. How the deuce they stand the pain I can't make out. The fellow stood up and looked at the shoe, asked again if it was the smallest they had and then said:

" 'Well, they'll do to roof the ranch-house with if they fall off my feet.' Cowboys don't like cigars. They like pipes, and are forever smoking them, but cigars they detest and don't know how to manage. Yet when they are flush, as they call it, and are engaged in buying out a tavern, they keep calling for cigars, and smoking a third or half of one only to throw it away and order fresh ones. The reason is that drinks and cigars are the only things on sale, and they feel obliged to buy something, whether they like it or not. The consequence is, if you go in a tavern some morning, after cowboys have spent a night in it, you will see the floor shoe-deep with cigars, not one of which has been half smoked. They are prodigiously fond of riding, and can't go from here to the corner on their feet; in fact, I have seen them mount their ponies merely to cross a street, time and time again."

During the journey through the grazing country the passengers on the train saw hundreds of cowboys, usually on horseback, riding on the prairie or in the towns. Some were picturesquely clad in broad, flapping sombreros and with fringed "chaps" of leather on their legs. Their saddles were the heavy, but pretty Mexican ones, made famous by all pictures of range life, and the lariat or lasso, coiled and hanging from the pommel, enhanced the picturesqueness of their appearance. Most of those who were seen, however, wore everyday costumes. Not one was dressed as they are gotten up on the stage or in the Wild West shows. They rode little horses, called cayooses in that country, because their fieryness and wiriness prompt the thought that they are a mongrel breed, blended of the native Indian pony and the coyote of the plains. These horses, and all else that distinguishes the cowboy life, are of Mexican origin. The cowboy dress, the "chaps," or chapparels, he wears as leggings, the whip he carries and calls his "quirt," his broad light-brown hat, his great spurs and heavy stirrups, his ornate saddle, his peculiar language all are Mexican, and all have followed his progress up from the first grazing plains of Mexico to those of Texas, and thus northward to the Canadian line. The cowboys are mainly from the Southern States the best of them from Tennessee and Kentucky though there are a few from the Eastern and Middle States. Almost all who have clung to the cowboy life spent their youth as farmers' sons. They lead a life of hard work and exposure, and are paid only $50 a month during eight months of the year. Important as they have been in the past, they will shortly become more so, for all signs point to the abandonment of the big ranches, and the cowboys are likely soon to become the only ranchmen, half herders and half farmers, for the grass is so short and the winter so severe that each ranchero must provide fodder against the days when snow will cover the plain. For years the most ambitious ones among the cow-punchers as they are called, in their own country have been establishing themselves in the business in small ways, and it looks as though the rich men who have of late been so disastrously pursued by bad luck in ranching will soon abandon the grazing country, leaving it dotted with small ranches owned by the men who used to be their assistants. **JULIAN RALPH.**

—A couple of Wyoming cowboys have had pistols made for them which cost $800 each. This is not strange when it is understood his revolver is the average cowboy's *sine qua non*, *vade mecum* and *E luribus unum*.

The *St. Joseph Weekly Gazette* (St. Joseph, Missouri) 17 Nov 1887.

# THE COWBOY'S VOCABULARY.

## Some of the Queer Words and Phrases Used in the West—Spanish Used Extensively.

*Kansas Pioneer* (Kansas City, Kansas) 17 Nov 1887. — The "Bucollo Dialect of the Plains" is made the subject of a paper by Louis Swinburne in the October number of Scribner's. Passing over the first page of his paper, which very interestingly traces the origin of the place names in the vicinity of the Rockies, we come, says *The Philadelphia Record*, to the class of words that have sprung up among cattle-owners and cowboys to designate the various acts and general conduct of their occupation, which the writer asserts have never been catalogued. The terms "rounding-up" and "branding" are too well known to be dealt upon. "Bucker," meaning a re-factory animal. Is also in ordinary use in the east being generally applied to refractory politicians. The cook on a ranch is called a "rustler," and the term is also applied to any uncommonly active man, and its sense has been still further amplified so that it may mean a thief. "Pilgrim" and "tenderfoot originally applied to newly imported cattle but now it means all newcomers whether two or four legged. "To go over the range" was also once limited to cattle, but now men as well as beasts that die "go over the range" in cowboy parlance. "Roped in" has also come to be of common use. Steers are "roped in" for the purpose of branding;

men are often "roped in" to their disadvantage. The epithet "thoroughbred" applied to a fine woman is very commonly used in the west but the English also use the word in the same sense.

The writer gives the following short list of ordinary cowboy words:

Brand, noun and verb; brand-book, containing the recorded brands of the country; branding-chute, branding-iron, counter-brand, v. and n,: flying-brand; lazy-brand; brand-bunch, small herd of cattle; bunch-grass; crease, v. n;. to stun a horse or steer by a blow in the neck in order to catch him; cutout to separate an animal from the herd; cutting-horse; crop, n. and v. an ear mark, or to make a mark by cutting the ear; dewlap, an out in the lower part of the neck; vent a brand announcing sale; single-bob, a slit ear dropping down. Other marks signifying ownership are over-bit, over-hack, over-half-crop, over-slope, swallow-fork, under-bit, under-back, etc. These are mostly technical, but the common terms are almost equally unfamiliar such as grade, adj. and n., improved cattle; grass-cattle, fed only on grass; hackamore, bridle made of horse-hair; heel, to lariat an animal by the hind leg; hondon (derivation unknown, though probably from Spanish honda, the eye of the needle), the slip-knot of the lariat; paunch, to shoot a refractory steer through the paunch, producing temporary quietude; slicker, a water-proof coat; string, a small collection of horses or steers; string-beam, pair of horses or mules in long succession; tall, to hold a steer down by the tall after it is lassoed and heeled; trail, n. and v. ; trail-cattle, trail-cinch; wrangler, a dog-herder; wrangle-footed, mixture of several gaits. The list is by no means complete, but it comprises the most common vernacular terms in use.

The class of words drawn from the Spanish is more numerous and more interesting. Ranch, from rancho, meaning mess, is commonly applied by the herder to his companions; so is "outfit;" vanios, to clear out; ranchoro is the steward of the mess; vaquero is the herder; companero, partner, and compadre, friend. The adobe of which the cowboy's house is built is known by its Spanish name alone. He calls his stove an estufa; eats tortillas, in other words hoocake; wears a serape (a light striped woolen shawl) over his shoulders; calls his fields of lucern fields of alfalfa, a dried-up creek an arrayos, deep holes made by the mountain flood barrancas, and water canals fused for Irrigation) acequras. Any collection of trees, brambles or bushes is a chaparral, and table-land is mesa. "Balie," corrupted into "bailee" among cowboys, is allied to our ball; but it mean's also sheriff (bailift), which is significant. The connection between balls and bailiffs in New Mexico is, unfortunately, more intimate and frequent than would be thought desirable in Boston and New York. The true cowboy delights in the lingering waits which the senoritas accord him. He will hop and roll about until he has worn out his zapatos (Spanish shoes), and still be is ready to swear that his partner is his ojo, the very eye of his heart.

Loco Is a Spanish word signifying mad, crack-brained. A plant of the plains which is poisonous to the cattle, producing symptoms of insanity, is called loco weed. "From the substantive a verb sprang into use. Cattle showing signs of madness are said to be 'locoed,' and so finally the word extended to human beings. Some have derived these meanings from the plant itself, as if it had originally borne the name loco; but this is incorrect the real process having been just the reverse of it.

Cuddy and burro are the two epithets which distinguish the small donkey. But the cowboy is getting to like the well-bred horse better, and the burro's day of popularity is gone. It is in relation to his horse and trappings that the cowboy's Spanish vocabulary is particularly rich. Preparatory to saddling, the hackamore, which is said to come from the Spanish jaquima, a halter, on the plains usually wrought of twisted hair, is thrown over his head and firmly tied. Then the saddle-blanket is over his withers, with sometimes a tilpah, or parti-colored rug, woven and died by the Navajo or Taos Indians; and over this the saddle, or perhaps the McClellan army-saddle. If it is the former it has to be "cinched." This is from the Spanish substantive chinca, meaning a bolt or girdle; chinchar, to girdle. To "cinch" a horse is by no means the same as girting him. The two ends of the tough cordage which constitute the "cinch" terminate in long, narrow strips of leather, called latigos (Spanish thongs), which connect the "cinches" with the saddle, and are run through an iron ring, called, if I remember correctly the larigo ring, though my deponent saith not and then tied by a series of complicated turns and knots. Sometimes there is a cource, or leather cover to protect the saddle. A pack saddle is an aparejo. The stout leather trousers for rough weather are called chaps, contracted from chaparro. A jacket of the same material is sometimes worn, cut short in the jaunty Spanish fashion, and braided, just as you see them in the streets of Seville. Add to these the woolen shirt gay in color and laced in front the high boots, the sash, and the great jingling spurs, and you have of the outer apparel of the borders nearly everything except the quirt the reata, the latigos and the tapaderos. Quirt is probably Spanish also, if we may now have to find its equivalent in cuerda, a rope; it is a short whip, made generally of dressed leather woven into many curious shapes. The ropes need to tie horses with is a lariat or convesta. Tapaderos and latigos are both applied to foot covering, and the cowboy never wears a hat, always a sombrero.

# Chapter 9: 1888

*"There is as much variety in this class as in any other calling of but as a rule all cowboys after becoming well broken to harness are gritty, full of dash and spirit, lively, brave to rashness, generous to a fault, and the very soul of honor and hospitality. Meet a "cowpuncher" alone on the prairie, and he will share his last crust and only blanket with you even before the asking."*

*- Memphis Daily Appeal*, 1888.

## HUNTING THE WILD HORSE

### A WESTERN SPORT IN WHICH RANCHMEN TAKE A LIVELY INTEREST.

The Wild Horse Chased and Shot as a Thief by Stock-Growers of the Far West—Coaxes His Domestic Brother Away from the Wagon and Plow to Taste Liberty in the Mountains—How the Indians Hunt Them—A Sport That Excels Buffalo Hunting.

Fort McKinney (Wyo.) Letter

***Chicago Tribune*** **(Chicago, Illinois) 05 Feb 1888.** — An immense black stallion lay dying on a hillside. His eyes were fast glazing over with the film of death as his blood slowly ebbed away from a bullet-hole in his lungs.

"There," said the old ranchman, as he stooped over the dying horse. "I guess you won't steal any more of my mares, you old rascal, you," and he contemptuously kicked the carcass. The ranchman was old Steine, a well-known horse-raiser in the Big Horn Mountains.

"What did you kill him for?" I asked.

"What did I kill him for?" said old Steine in astonishment. "For stealing my mares, of course. You didn't suppose I killed him for fun, did ye?"

"I didn't know," I replied modestly, "but it seems a pity to kill so fine a beast."

"A fine old thief," said Steine, kicking the carcass again. "Why, man, do you know that old cuss has stolen more than a dozen of my mares, and I reckon $1,000 wouldn't pay for the damage he has done in this valley during the last summer."

"Tell me all about it," I said, "for it all seems very strange to me."

"I reckon it wouldn't seem very strange to you, stranger, if you lived up in these parts and were a trying to raise horses." And the man smiled at me contemptuously, as if he thought I was a greenhorn just out from the East.

"See here, old man," I said, sharply, "I'll thank you not to take me for a tenderfoot, for I reckon I have been on the plains as long as you have, but I never saw anybody kill a horse like that before."

"Guess your experience at horse-raising, then, is rather limited, stranger," said old Steine, "but as you ask me a civil question and seem to be an honest sort of a chap I'll tell you all about it." "Didn't you never hear of wild horses," he asked, suddenly. "Yes," I said, "I have, of course."

"Well," continued Steine, "that's one of them lying there, and I reckon he was the biggest thief in the whole lot. You see, they run in gangs of fifty to a hundred, and the stallions steal our mares and drive them off into the wild bands, and that's the last we ever see of them unless it is with a spy-glass. They just go plum wild, and seem worse nor the real Wild mares."

I then learned from the old ranchman some curious facts about the wild horses of the plains. Every effort to destroy them has proved futile, and the aid of the Territorial Government is now to be asked to eradicate their bands. They have increased so wonderfully within the last few years that they have become an unbearable nuisance to the stock-growers of the plains. They graze in bands of twenty, fifty, and even 100, and are very difficult to approach. An old stallion generally occupies some elevation, and he will trumpet an alarm to the herd if he sees any one coming. In times of danger from wild beasts the stallions form a circle and the mares and colts are put inside. The colts are often attacked by wolves or Rocky Mountain lions, but they never succeed in killing a colt without a battle with the horses, and often the wolves and lions are kicked and beaten so badly that they have to beat a retreat without securing their prey. The stallions are regular Mormons, and get all the mares they can. They cross and recross the country looking for mares, and even proselyting for horses to enter their band. If cow ponies stray too far from the cattle or camp the first thing they know they are rounded up by an old stallion and driven off into the hills. Often a wild herd will discover a tame band of horses grazing quietly in the valley with no intention of leaving their range but the band of wild horses, led on by their stallions, dash down into the valley capture them, and carry them away. The wild stallions are shot without mercy by the ranchmen. If one is seen grazing on a hill he is sneaked upon and dropped in his tracks. They are very alert and difficult to approach, but, like the tame horse, are easily killed. A bullet in almost any part of the body will cause the horse to drop on the plain.

The Indians are the best wild-horse hunters, but they do not like to be out in stormy weather, and they cannot stand the cold of winter as well as white men. In a storm is the best time to hunt wild horses, for then they bunch, and cannot see any one approaching until it is too late to get out of the way of the bullets. It is generally useless for a hunter to attempt to run down a wild horse with a tame one. The tame horse, weighted down by the burden of the hunter's body, soon tires, and the wild horse easily escapes. Sometimes the hunters discover the tracks of wild horses near a stream, and they then hunt for their watering place. The band always water at the same place, and, although right on the stream, the horses will go up or down it for a mile or more in order to drink at their accustomed watering place. Hiding in the brush or crawling to a bluff, the hunter lies in wait until the horses come to the water and then shoots them. It is difficult to catch them, as they seem to know instinctively when hunters are about, and if they even suspect danger they will at once leave the locality. A smoke or anything unusual will stampede them, and they will run forty or fifty miles before letting up. Their sense of smell is very acute, and on the wind side about a mile is as close as a hunter can get before being discovered by his odor, and the horses are off in a jiffy.

The winter is the best season for wild horse hunting in Wyoming. The animals get discouraged by the deep snows and become hungry and poor. They are apt at such times to bunch in the cottonwood groves, where they eat the bark off the trees and chew up all the small limbs they can reach. Sometimes in the summer-time the cowboys make up large parties and go out to hunt wild colts. On such occasions they take their lassoes, some good riding horses, and provisions, and hunt for the band. A band sighted, they creep up under cover as near as possible, and then, mounting, give chase. The colts, being weak, soon fall behind the band and are lassoed and choked into submission. The little fellows are not hard to conquer, and when separated from their wild companions domesticate easily, but can never be trusted. A band of cowboys had some colts in camp and they became so tame they turned them loose with the other horses. They staid about for a day or two, but one morning they were missing and were never seen again.

A farmer who had a wild colt given to him by a cowboy put it in a lot by his house and kept it there a long time. It became so tame it would eat sugar out of his hand and let him fondle it. One day he left the bars down by accident, and in the evening it was missing. It was seen several miles from home and pursued, but it escaped to the mountains and never came back.

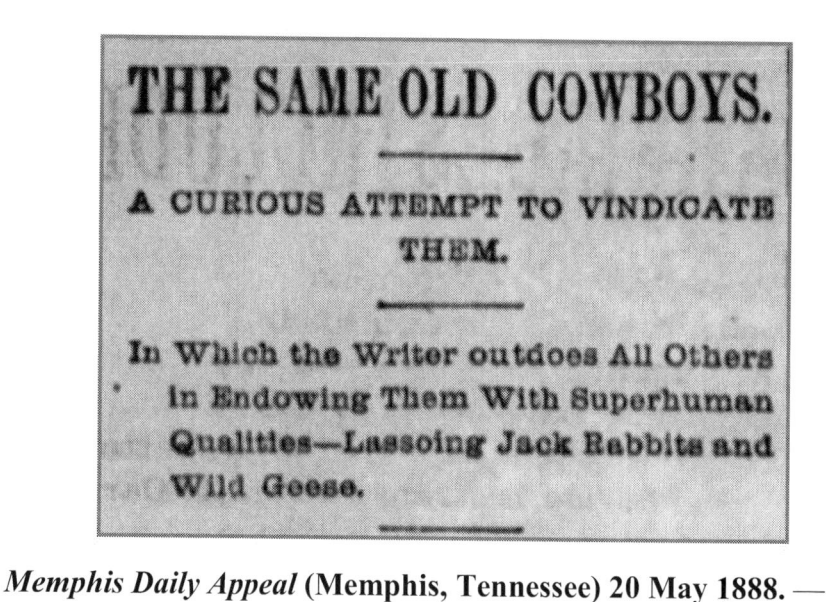

## THE SAME OLD COWBOYS.

### A CURIOUS ATTEMPT TO VINDICATE THEM.

In Which the Writer outdoes All Others in Endowing Them With Superhuman Qualities—Lassoing Jack Rabbits and Wild Geese.

*Memphis Daily Appeal* (**Memphis, Tennessee**) **20 May 1888.** — Miles City Correspondence of the New York Times. The ordinary cowboy of the west, and particularly of the northwest, is the most thoroughly understood man on the face of earth. Eastern people imagine that all carry one or more revolvers apiece, ride fiery, untamed mustangs, wear broad sombreros with half-acre brims and rattlesnake bands, are filled to overflowing with profanity and fun, are ready to shoot on drop of a hat if not sooner, and are altogether on a par with the blood and thunder characters portrayed in flashy literature. As a matter of fact the cowboy of nature is no such thing. There is as much variety in this class as in any other calling of but as a rule all cowboys after becoming well broken to harness are gritty, full of dash and spirit, lively, brave to rashness, generous to a fault, and the very soul of honor and hospitality. Meet a "cowpuncher" alone on the prairie, and he will share his last crust and only blanket with you even before the asking.

Miles City is the cowboy headquarters of the northwest. Here every variety of the type can be met with during the round-up season. One can jostle upon the street corners men who are veritable cowboys in every sense of the word; men who personally accompany the round-ups, cut out cattle, lariat steers, and sleep on the open prairie with a saddle for a pillow and the starry canopy for a coverlet; and yet those very men, some of whom are scarcely able to write their own names, could buy and sell many of our so called millionaire nabobs of eastern cities. One class of cowboys are college bred men, or sons of college men, who follow the calling for health and not wealth. Somehow they manage to secure both health and wealth, when really in need of only the former. A lady whose home ranch is in this neighborhood was sitting on the portico of a hotel in Miles City recently waiting for her husband to come in from the ranch. She had just arrived from "the States," and had brought with her a friend, a young woman, who was anxious to see the western life. The visitor had never met the husband or any relative of her hostess. All at once around the corner of the street came dashing at almost breakneck speed two cowboys mounted on plains cayuses. They were dressed according to rule — leather trousers, flannel shirts, Texas sombreros and top boots.

"Oh, my!" exclaimed the horrified visitor, "just look at that horrid cowboy. See his greasy trousers, big pistols and muddy boots. Ugh! Let's go in."

"Why that's my husband," said her companion quietly. "No, not that one," quickly responded the lady, flushing crimson. "I meant the other." "Why, that's my brother."

Matters have so far progressed favorably since the visitor from the east met these two cowboys that she is likely soon to become the wife of one of them. Moral: A remarkable change comes over a man, outwardly, when he dons his swallow-tail coat in New York and comes out west and dons a herder's suit of leather on the plains.

Another class of plains herders are a mad sort, to say the least, who are headstrong, plucky, and always ready for fun of any description and perpetually on the watch to startle out of his five senses any unsophisticated tenderfoot fresh from the east who chances to come along. Still have they a reckless generosity and rough kind-heartedness wound in among all their faults which softens their nature and prevents them from being a hundredth part as cruel as they outwardly seem to be.

The Northern Pacific railroad cuts directly through the great cattle range of the northwest. Passengers on these trains are always on the watch to catch a glimpse of a genuine cowboy, and you may be sure that the boys never let an opportunity slip by to startle and horrify these innocents, who are making their first journey to the land of the setting sun.  In the Bad Lands of Dakota are the ranches of the cowboy nobleman, the Marquis de Mores, Theodore Roosevelt, and many other prominent men, whose herds roam at will over the vast free ranges of the northwest.  The style of cowboys at Medora (capital of the Bad Lands certainly eclipse anything of the kind elsewhere on the continent.  For reckless daring and useless exploits of a marvelous sort these lads have a reputation second to none.  Scarcely a train sweeps through the wonderful Bad Lands but ten or a dozen cowboys mounted on the worst of bucking and racing cayuse bronchos, are cutting all sorts of capers and giving a general free circus for the edification and amusement of the wondering passengers, who possibly have never seen such sights before.  Such exhibitions of equestrianism the astonished tenderfeet never dreamed of.  Just at Medora is the Little Missouri river, spanned by a trestle bridge more than 100 feet above the water.   In the center, upon the ties, runs a narrow plank walk used by the railroad footmen, and it requires a level head and steady nerves event for a sober man to make the long trip successfully from shore to shore.  A train loaded with passengers had stopped at a water tank for a few minutes just before crossing the bridge and staring tourists were gaping in open-eyed wonder at a dozen or more cowpunchers who were cavorting about and doing all sorts of impossible things on horseback.  One of them would set a broncho to bucking with all his might and then in a twinkling "bust him." Another would throw his beast and leap nimbly out of danger. Another yet would make an extraordinary leaps, a third or fourth pick up pebbles from the ground while going at full speed, a fifth and sixth would have their steeds quietly back on their haunches, sitting up like so many dogs, while others would be handling the rope — lassoing trees, stones, dogs, Pullman porters, each other, and in fact anything within reach.

All at once the locomotive snorted up and spurted a little stream preparatory to pushing across the bridge and out into the unknown west. Here was a chance, and two of the most daring of the cow-punchers lost no time in seizing the opportunity. Lying, almost flat on the necks of their steeds they drove their cruel spur into the flanks of their cayuses, and started on a hop, skip and jump across the bridge ahead of the locomotive. It was a mad chase never to I forgotten by the onlookers. The spectators were thrilled with the horror. The two horsemen in single file were fairly flying along the narrow plank walk, and hot on their heels came the steaming locomotive. Everyone expected to see the daring riders dashed to death at every jump, or else overtaken and crushed by the pursuing train, but neither casualty occurred. The reckless fellows yelled vociferously to their steeds and rode with the same easy confidence as if on the open prairie and chasing cattle on a round up. The race was a short one, it is needless to say, and was won by the cowboy. When they came out on terra firma some yards ahead of the locomotive a shout went up from the throats of all who had witnessed the fun, and the engine added it acclamation in a series of shrill screeches that were echoed and re-echoed back from the buttes of the Bad Lands in 1,000 reverberations.

The skill of the genuine cowboy in handling a rope cannot be questioned. Marvelous stories get abroad through the eastern press reciting most astonishing feats of prowess, in which the "lads of the plain" get credit for performing what would seem to do next to impossible. As a matter of fact, not half the truth has been told regarding the genuine, bona fide exploits of those sons of the prairie. Dick Rock, the ne plus ultra of cayuse riders, actually did, on a wager, leap astride the back of a live buffalo and ride him for many miles without saddle or bridle. The feat was performed in the presence of witnesses over in Red Water country, about sixty-five miles north of this point. Another cowboy — Dan Farley, I believe his name is — had ridden across the country to bid some of his friends good-by who were leaving on a train. When the train pulled away from the station and had about one quarter mile started Farley discovered he had left his overcoat aboard. Then began a race between steam and horseflesh that has seldom, if ever, seen before. Away went the cowpuncher like the wind over coalers, through sage brush, and smashing prairie-dog towns, or rather domiciles, right and left. It was a hard run, but the cayuse came out a winner. The train was overtaken within a mile and a half and the overcoat thrown out of a window by the watching friend.

As lariat swingers the cowboys of the northwest cannot be approached by the Mexican or Arizona vaquero, nor by any other of their relations in Texas or elsewhere in the south. It is all very well to rope and throw a 1,000 pound steer, to catch him by the horns or hoof at will and make a prisoner of the big fellow, but when it comes to lassoing mountain lions, elk, antelope, bears and even flying geese, the gentlemanly "slingers" from the southern ranges will have to acknowledge the superiority of their northern brethren. Casting a noose over the horns of an infuriated steer is a most insignificant performance for them. With the utmost ease those northwestern heroes will catch an animal anywhere that is, where it can be caught and so throw a 1,200 or 1,500 pounder with the utmost ease. Red Carian, a puncher working with the Green Mountain Cattle company on the South Yellowstone range, not long since succeeded in casting a noose over the head of a monster mountain lion. The animal was surprised and belligerent when he found the coils of a half-inch rope settling slightly down over his collar bone, and he would no doubt have made it quite lively for Mr. Carian had not the cowboy's friends come to his relief and caught the lion on the hip, so to speak, by lariating him from an opposite side of the compass. As it was, the monarch of mountain solitude was made a prisoner beyond all hope of rescue, and was pounded to death with rock from the hand of other of the party. On the Snake river, a short time ago, a ferryboat crossing the rapid stream broke her cable and started toward the frightful Shoshone falls, only thirty miles away. One passenger was aboard, Thomas Starrh and he seemed to be beyond hope, for no rescue could reach him in the middle of a rapid, turbulent stream that was unnavigable for craft of any kind. Mr. Starrh had about resigned himself to his fate. When the boat passed Snoddy's cattle ranch the cowboys espied her. Hurrying to the shore, half a dozen experts soon had their lariats swinging, and one, more fortunate than the rest, succeeded in casting his rope across the boat Mr. Starrh instantly made the line fast, and the boat completely and cleverly captured, swung around in the stream and was pulled to the shore.

During the fall round-up of last year three Montana cowboys over on Big Crooked creek, while riding the ranges in search of lost stork, ran upon a huge silver-tip bear who was quietly nosing around among the berry bushes on the bank of the stream. Without a thought as to consequences the three reckless men gave chase to the bear, who started westward briskly. It was a foolhardy attempt in the extreme, for the pursuers were without arms, only possessing long and strong sinewy lariats; still they resolved to capture the bear. Gudgel, Reid and Jones held a consultation for a moment, in which it was determined to lasso the beast while going at full speed. Approaching within casting distance, at the word three nooses went sailing through the air, two of which hit the bull's-eye. One shot was to catch the bear by the neck, another by a fore-foot, and the third by the hind leg. Foot lariating is a most difficult calculation to make, for the loop must fall on the spot where the animal will place his paw and the draw must be made instantaneously, else there can be no catch. One loop went all right over his head, the magic circle fell exactly correct for the left hind leg, but the foreleg cast was a failure. At any rate, the burly fellow was a pioneer from two causes, and this was enough, both cowboys stopping at once, the bear was thrown from his feet and went rolling head over heels in the dust. In a twinkling, however, he was up again and going for the enemies hammer-and-tongs style. He fought desperately to relieve himself, and although caught afoul from two quarters he dragged one of his captors, horse and all some feet, far enough to catch Reid's horse by the tail and draw from the astonished animal's caudal appendage a whole mouthful of hair. Jones, who had missed a strike in the first instance, now succeeded in catching the bear by a fore leg. In this position the poor animal was worked skillfully up a coulisse and one rope made fast to a tree. Then Gudgel mauled Mr. Bear with rocks. It was a hard tussle without arms, but the olds were too great against the silver tip, even with no other weapons than a simple lariat. In the Medora Bad Lands is a roving spirit named Henry Williams. Williams is in the employ of the Neimmella Cattle company, on the Little Missouri river, and one day last season, with a grass rope in his hands actually succeeded in roping a wild goose on the wing. He had been hunting some missing horses, and had come across two or three of the animals drinking at the river. He rode down to turn them out when a full grown wild goose flew in from under a bunch of sage brush on the river's bank and passed straight in front of him. He had his rope uncoiled and ready for use. with which he intended to drive, the horse out of the river, and. quick a thought while the bird was darting past him, he launched the rope into the air and caught the goose by the left wing.

The air was filled with honks for a few seconds, but protest was useless, as the goose was prisoner. Williams took the bird home with him, but it soon died in captivity. Jess Reeves, one of our cowboys and a wonderful expert with the lariat, actually succeeded in capturing singly and securely a jack rabbit going across the prairie at railroad speed.

> Captain Jack Lyons, the Champion Colorado cowboy, will give a grand exhibition of mustang riding, lassooing wild cattle and horses, and other daring feats on the mustangs back, at Barrell Springs, July 4th, 1888.

The *Colokan Graphic* (Colokan, Kansas) 8 Jun 1888.

# Chapter 10: 1889

*"The owner of the ranch is the cattleman, the employee whatever his age may be, the cowboy."*

-Cromwell Childe, 1889.

## FACTS ABOUT COWBOYS.

The *Perry Daily Chief* (Perry, Iowa) 4 Jan 1889. —

### They Are Very Hard on Horses and Generally Very Poor Shots

"I have lived among the cowboys for many years," said Mr. Gosnold of Laredo, Tex., who has lived on the frontier since 1853, "and think I know them thoroughly. I find that a general impression prevails throughout the country that they are phenomenal horsemen and good shots. Neither of these opinions is correct. Although all have foundations in fact. First, as to their horsemanship, as far as sticking on and understanding what can be done in the saddle goes, they certainly are second to no riders in the world. For a Texas cowboy to pick up a hat or silver dollar from the ground when at full speed, to mount his horse at the gallop, or to stop him in full career, and turn him on a saddle blanket, are every-day feats. The best of the riders can stand on the saddle of a galloping horse, or pick up a coin lying on the ground on the left side of the horse with the right hand, a most difficult feat, and one and all can ride bucking horses. But here their horsemanship ends, and beyond this are worse than the veriest tryo, because the cowboys have faults which the most ordinary park rider of the East is free. I will venture say that if one thousand Texans start a long march, where speed is necessary, side by side with a United States regiment, the latter will reach destination long before the former, and have its stock in serviceable condition, while the Texas horses will be only for the bone yard. Men understanding less about horses and less to keep their mounts in good condition it would be hard to find. Accustomed to a superabundance of horses, they never undertake either to train or spare them, and would break down the best horse in American in a week. Although their horses are small a saddle weighing from thirty to pounds is used, the most of this weight being useless leather. When one bears in mind the old racing saying that the weight of a stable key will win or lose a race, the absurdity of this style of saddle is apparent. During the war the value of Texans as was well proved. They were greatly relied upon and much dreaded, but when they came before the enemy after a march of two or three hundred miles not one horse in five was in serviceable condition, and the entire force was worse than useless. Then they thought they knew every thing about riding, and refused to receive instructions. It being impossible to make them into as good as the rawest recruits became after a few months' training. It is practically impossible for a horse throw them, but outside of this they are the most destructive and riders in the world.

"As to their shooting." continued Gosnold, "because every man used a revolver and was ready to use it people supposed they were fine shots. One thing they did understand and that was quick shooting, but as to any accuracy, not one in a hundred possessed it. Pistol combats in Texas wear nearly always of the shoulder to kind, where speed was of far importance than aim, and a Texan could fire a great number of in a given time. But when it to came to fine marksmanship, they were nowhere, and in an Eastern shooting gallery would not begin to be able to hold their own. As rifle shots they are even worse, and could not hold any position at all in Creedmoor or any regular rifle range." — St*. Louis Dispatch.*

## THE COWBOY'S OUTFIT.

### A FEATURE OF FRONTIER LIFE FAST DISAPPEARING.

*Deerfield Valley Times* **(Wilmington, Vermont) 4 Apr 1889.** — People all over Western Kansas and No Man's Land are full of stories and reminiscence of cowboy life. In fact, a plenty of the citizens of these Western villages served as cowboys at one time and another before they became merchants, professional men, etc., in some favorite location for a town site. One hears on every hand expressions that were technical in the cowboys' camp. Landlord Osgood calls his guests to breakfast in the morning with the song that the cowboy sings while riding around his cattle at night to keep them from getting frightened and stampeding thus:

Hay-a-a-a-a — Y-o-o-o-o — Hay-a-a-a-a — Y-o-o-o-o — Breakfast. When anything is tied up it is said to be roped, from the term which the cowboy applied to the use of the lasso. A man's household goods are termed an outfit. So is his kit of tools, if a mechanic; his library and appliances, if a surgeon or lawyer; his safe, desks, etc., if a banker. So, too, is the clique he associates with socially. He belongs to a poker outfit if he plays cards with regularity, or to a pious outfit if he goes to church. People in the East have often read of the cowboy when on a spree "shooting up the town" or lynching a horsethief, but not very many know anything about the real life of the cowboy, and of what his outfit is compose or what it costs. The most important article in the cowboy's outfit is the chuck wagon, or the wagon over which the cook presides. It is a common prairie schooner, with hoops over it to stretch a canvas roof on, so that such a perishable goods as salt sugar and flour can be protected from the weather. At the back is a cupboard, where such thing as baking powder, pepper, coffee, dishes, etc., are kept. There are pots and frying pans a plenty, and the larder is always well supplied. Bacon is generally preferred to salt pork, and fresh beef is kept constantly on hand by killing a steer from the herd as occasion requires. The owners of the herd supply the food, and such tools as shovels, axes, etc. The shovel, it is interesting to know, is generally of much more use than the axe. When taking a wagon across the streams it is very often necessary to cut down the banks on either side to form an inclined plane, for perpendicular banks three and four feet high are common. Then, too the streams very often run under ground. The bed of a creek may be covered with sand and gravel burning hot, by digging two or three feet — sometimes as much as six or eight — pure, sweet water may be had in abundance.

    Timber for fuel may be had in some parts of the range and not in others, but when it is abundant the cowboy's cook generally prefers the ancient buffalo chips, which he calls Kansas or prairie coal. Next to the chuck wagon among the needs of the cowboy is his pony. The Texas pony is a marvel to an Eastern man. It weighs from 500 to 600 pounds only, but it canters away for forty or fifty miles with a well-grown man, say from 150-170 pounds weight, on its back, and then rustles for its feed and comes up fresh for another canter of the same length next day. The cowboys tell of much greater feats of strength and endurance than this, but the Sun reporter saw this much done.

Each cowboy, however is supplied with six ponies by the owner, because while a pony can stand several days of hard riding in succession, it is more economical to have several on hand and give each a chance to rest between rides. The ponies are worth only from $20 to $30 each, they are a vicious lot and buck ecstatically every time they are mounted. The cowman supplies the cowboy with four blankets, saddle, bridle, and lasso, as well as ponies, but the cowboy who has any style about him scorns both the saddle and the lasso furnished by the company. The company's saddle is simply a substantial skeleton costing not more than $10. The cowboy buys his own, and it costs $50 at least. It is made of stamped and embroidered leather, and everything about it is of the very best quality. One firm in Wichita, Kansas, has made a great fortune by first making the very best saddle that can be made by human skill, and then charging these prices for it. The cowboy pays the price because he is sure of getting the best saddle made.

The company lasso is made of rawhide. It cost $10. It does very well in fine weather; in a rainstorm it is stiff and awkward to handle. The cowboy leaves it with the outfit, and takes his own. This is made of horsehair, and is always as flexible as a bit of cotton twine and strong enough to hold an elephant. It has a range in the hands of a man of skill of sixty feet the noose can be dropped over a steer's horns at that distance. Its costs the cowboy from $30 to $33. To learn to use the lasso requires constant practice for from four week to six months, according to the individual of course, some men never become experts, while others seem to be "born with ropes in their hands."

Other essentials of the cowboy outfit are the repeating rifle and the six shooter. A good rifle costs $35 and a good six shooter but little less. The cowboy must have ivory or other fancy handles, and the mountings must be of gold and silver. But this weapon, although fancy, is deadly in the right hands. The Eastern man comes here expecting to find every cowboy an expert with the revolver, and is somewhat astonished to find that not one in ten can be so classed. The reputation of the few clings to the whole. One of the best revolver shots in the Indian Territory is Dave Geber, a half breed living with the Peorias. He can hit a target the size of a man's head six times in rapid succession while riding his pony at full speed at a distance of 200 yards. Having learned to shoot while riding on horseback, he cannot shoot so well standing on foot and aiming deliberately, and that is one of the peculiarities of the cowboy marksman. To return to the pony trappings, the spurs of a cowboy are worth mentioning. A cheap pair made of maleable cast iron can be bought for twenty-five cents. The fancy spurs cost from $2 to $5 a pair. They are plated with silver, and engraved in fancy designs, sometimes, but the part to which the cowboy directs his attention when buying is the rowel or wheel, and the bell. The wheel must have long and substantial spokes. The bell is a little piece of steel shaped like the clapper of a Bell. It is secured to the fork that holds the rowel. For business purposes it is dropped in between two spokes of the rowel and thus prevents the rowell turning. Having done this, the cowboy can drop down over the side of his pony, catching the rowel in his saddle to support one end of his body, hanging to the pommel with one hand to support the other, and working the trigger of his six-shooter under the neck of his pony to make things interesting for the enemy. In the days when Indians were in the habit of stampeding herds at every opportunity the rowel and bell were of great importance in a running fight. The article of wearing apparel which is the pride of the cowboy's heart is his hat. A good broad-brimmed hat cannot be bought for less than $6. The very best cost $20. That is for the hat. The hat band is bought extra. A leather band with a clinking brass chain attached may be had for a dollar. A cord of braided gold lace, such as a cowboy would wear in society, costs from $7.50 to $10. City Recorder George A. Blake, of Beaver City, No Man's Land, wears a head outfit that cost $37.50, of which the braided-gold cord cost $7.50. Rube Chilcott, who runs the Beaver livery stable, has another hat and band of the same sort. Both men were once cowboys. But it is not altogether as a matter of fancy that expensive hats are bought. The broad brim is a great protection to the back of the neck and the face when riding in a storm across the range. A storm on the range is like a gale at sea. The wind sweeps unimpeded over the level prairie, and drives the rain or snow against the cowboy almost with the force of a charge of birdshot. The best hat — the one that is at once warm and waterproof is good enough on such occasions, but none too good.

Next to his hat the cowboy is proud of his boots. They must be handmade, of the best and softest of leather, and they must have long legs, and heels that will throw the French heel of a lady's boot entirely in the shade. Heels from an inch to an inch and a quarter high are the proper thing for cowboys who wish to attend a dance in this country. Boots of this sort cost from $13 to $15.

Singular enough, the cowboy cares as little for the quality of his suit of clothes as he does about the cost of his pony. A $13 suit of store clothes, such as would cost say $9 in New York, are good enough for him, while his suit of flannels will not cost above $4. In some parts of the country, leather trousers that are laced, instead of sewed up, on the outer seams, are in use. They cost from $6 to $7 a pair, and are valued because they wear well, and because snakes cannot bite through them. Then, too, the cowboy usually has a pair of slickers. Slickers are called oilskins by seafaring men. They are made of duck, and are made waterproof by a soaking in oil.
As might be inferred, from what has been written, the bill of fare of the cowboy consists chiefly of bread and bacon and beef and coffee. Butter and milk are almost unknown, although there are thousands of cows on the range. George Blake told the reporter, however, that on a range where he was in charge he fitted up a milk house over a spring near where the outfit had its headquarters, and having bought a churn and some pans, kept the outfit supplied with butter and sweet milk. Every outfit might be supplied but for the dislike of milking which every cowboy evinces.

The diet of beef and pork is always varied with game, too. There is generally one shot gun with the outfit for prairie chickens, while deer, antelope, and jack rabbits are shot in numbers with rifles and six-shooters. Out of ten men in the Saginaw outfit, Dave Geber said at least two went hunting every Sunday. The daily experience of the cowboy is monotonous in most respects, but not unfrequently he has enough excitement in fifteen minutes to last most men a lifetime. By day he must keep the cattle moving slowly about so that they will have some exercise. One herd of 800 in the Peoria reservation, which the reporter saw, had a range of ten miles. They were driven over the most of this and back once a day. At night when the cattle lie down to sleep a small bunch like the 800 will be left to care for itself. With a herd like the Saginaw Company's, 8,500 strong, two men rode constantly around the herd all night singing in a monotonous chant Hay-a-a-e-Yo-o-o-o-o, Hay-a-a-a-Yo-o-o-o-o. To stop for a minute was extremely dangerous, for the cattle, missing the song to which they were accustomed, would become uneasy. The cowboys stand watches of two hours' length at night.

 Sometimes through carelessness, but often in spite of care, the cattle will become alarmed. It is as if they saw a ghost, the cowboys say. In an instant there are thousands on their feet, and away they go in a mad gallop, straight to destruction, if they cannot be turned. This is the moment that tries the nerve of the cowboy. He must get them to circling — running in a circle — and there is but one way to do it.

They will blindly follow a leader, and he must be that leader. Spurring his pony into a wilder gallop than that of the cattle, he must ride in ahead of the frightened herd and continue without a tremor in his voice his song of "Hay-a-a-a-yo-o-o-o-o; hay-a-a-a-yo-o-o-o-o," even though it is his own death knell, for should his pony slip on the wet grass, or put its foot in the hole of a badger or a prairie dog, he will go down under the feet of the frightened cattle and have the life trampled out of him before he has time to think. A good many cowboys have died that way, they say, but no one has ever thought of erecting a monument over their graves. Sometimes there are cattle in the herd that will not follow the cowboy leader as he strives to make them circle. These tangents, as they are called, must be shot down instantly, and is for this reason that the cowboy must learn to handle the six shooter as well as the lariat. The cowboy generally sleeps in the open air. He may crawl under a chuck wagon in case of rain, but he usually sleeps out. Where the cattle remain in a definite locality for a length of time he may build a house or shanty where there is timber. Tents are used sometimes. The kings of the craft get $50 and even $75 a month. The tenderfoot starts in at whatever he can get — $10 or $13 or $15 a month. — *New York Sun.*

# THE COWBOY VINDICATED.

## THE TEXAS COWBOY OF YESTERDAY IS THE CATTLE KING OF TODAY.

A Much Maligned Individual Whose Portrait Has Been Distorted by the Eastern Imagination—He Is Generally Highly Educated and High-Minded, and a Disorderly Character Is Exceptional—The Drivers Who Visit Chicago Are Not Real Cowboys.

*Chicago Tribune* (Chicago, Illinois) 28 Apr 1889. — There is probably no class about which so much pure fiction has been written, and believed, as about the Texas cowboy. I say Texas cowboy because it was the Texas cowboy who first made that name famous. The Eastern press has given him, in the minds of the people, his fictitious character. These pictures of him, have given the world the most gorgeous idea as to what kind of per son he is.

The Eastern and remote periodicals have illustrated him as a person going about with a Winchester slung to his back, four huge revolvers in his belt, and a long bowie knife in each boot leg a regular walking arsenal. The artists have fitted him up in clothes which would make an ancient Comanche warrior ashamed of his lack of picturesque savagery in dress. This Eastern cowboy picture, or Eastern picture of a Texas cowboy, always has a hat with a brim as large as the dome on the Mormon Temple, a woolen overshirt, open in front, with fancy flowers embroidered on it, and twilled silk cord in lieu of buttons and with tassels at the ends.

Eastern periodicals describe him as having a countenance like a pirate, uncombed hair, a face which has been for months a stranger alike to either razor or soap, and with leather breeches on when he goes to see his "best girl," or goes to a dance or to church, both of which latter places he is said to regard as places especially organized for his amusement when he is not on duty. He is always described as reckless of human life and generally pictured in the "taking-in-the-town" illustrations as piling up a lot of dead men on the floor or in front of the places where objection is made to his free and easy style of fun. Now, the truth is, the Eastern man would not recognize a Texas cowboy were he to see one even out on a drive, not to mention if he were to meet one in town. I was a traveling correspondent for an Eastern paper down in Texas and Mexico for over fifteen years, and never saw a single cowboy like those I had always read about and seen illustrated. I first thought this strange. But I no longer think so. People, must have, what they want, and they seemed to want the Texas cowboy pictured so he would be a monstrosity, as in keeping with the tough name Texas had acquired from her frontier situation. And he got that name, too. He is a different individual in real life, and a unique and interesting one. To begin with, he is frequently a scholar. I remember in 1874, when I was following Col. Fred Grant as correspondent for my paper, to have examined the diplomas of 63 young men out in Wise, Clay, and Hardeman Counties, Texas, out of

103 cowboys. And those diplomas were from such universities as Harvard, Yale, Princeton, the University of Virginia, and the leading institutions of the land. These young men had gone out to try their fortunes, some with ample means to start for themselves when they had learned the business, for it must be thoroughly learned to attain success; some of them for their health, and many to get a start. And at the cattlemen's conventions here I meet many of those same cowboys of fifteen years ago who are now cattle-kings and known as men of culture and wealth, and who are sought after socially. The Texas cowboy is almost always a gentleman. I do not mean that he always has the polish of a Chesterfield or the acquired suavity in mode of an Admirable Crichton. I mean that he is gallant, quick to respond to every appeal for assistance, the avowed slave and defender of a woman's name and honor, never forgetting that the sex of his mother and sisters should have his reverence and respect whether clothed in the simple garb of the lowly or the silken robes of wealth and fashion. And he is not so awkward in a drawing-room as one would suppose, as he sees there more frequently than some of those who would caricature him.

## HIS PECULIAR DRESS.

On the trail the cowboy is rough of dress. He would be an idiot were he to dress in any other manner. Going through brush and thorns, and out in rain and storm as he has to do, the cowboy needs clothing which will not tear and will turn water and keep out cold or heat. The hide of cows and horses, and goats, dressed with the hair out, serves both purposes, and the Texas cowboy adopted this as a kind of overalls to put on over his pants. He wears a broad brimmed hat, so as to protect him from the sun and the rain. He doesn't wear tremendous spurs at all. Sometimes he doesn't wear any. If he aces, they are a small pair with short rowels, and seldom used. He prefers his Mexican quirt, a small, plaited riding whip with fancy knots and twists made on the handle. His boots are the most unique thing about his appearance. And when he is off duty, and in town on what might be called dress parade, these boots mark out the Texas cowboy more than any other part of his attire, except, perhaps, his diamond rings, or pins, if they might be called attire. These boots are made to order and are never cheap. They are usually small, as most of the Texas cowboys have small feet. This fact will be new to many and sound incredible. But it is the truth. Take any number of Texas cowboys and you will find that, while they will be average sized men, their boots will range in size from 4s to 6s on an, average. The conspicuous part of them is their boot heels. They have high and small heels, which are slanted forward till they almost reach under the middle of the foot. This peculiar make of boot is a purely Texas cowboy style, I believe. I find dealers so class them, and Eastern shoe houses have told me that they have no considerable trade on such anywhere except in Texas. They make this kind especially for the Texas trade for the most part. And in Texas no one wears them but the cowboy or his cousin, the real Texas farm boy who gets his idea of dandyism from the cowboy because of the latter's supposed advantages in the way of knowing how to dress, acquired from having been "around among the people." The Texas cowboy is not a shooter of men. He carries a six-shooter when he is away out on the trail where the professional cattle thieves and the Mexican and Indian robbers hold full sway. But he never carries it in his belt when he goes into a city or town. You will find 75 per cent more pistols carried among the "bon ton" citizens of the large cities than you will among any company of Texas cowboys in a city or town. They never did go armed in towns except on the extreme frontier, where they were m danger of encountering rival herders who wanted a row amongst themselves. The cowboy carries a Winchester rifle on the trail, but it is slung under his right stirrup in a leather "scabbard." True, once in a while a cowboy does go into a town, get drunk, and shoot around, maybe shooting through a window or doing some other damage. But he doesn't hurt any one, and he is almost invariably arrested, his companions helping to turn him over to the authorities and paying his fine next morning, and then they give him a "cussin' " for being such a fool. This kind of a cowboy is the exception, really.

### HIS ACCOMPLISHMENTS.

It is in his skill with the lasso and his horsemanship, as well as his accuracy of aim with a pistol or rifle while going at full gallop, that the Texas cowboy is preeminent. And it is his proficiency in these which has aided in giving him the terrible name he bears, no doubt. The romantic name of the Aztec as a horseman and a thrower of the lasso pales before the accomplishments of the Texas cowboy in those feats. He carries his lasso coded ready for instant use, and fastened to the horn (pummel) of his saddle with a buckskin string so looped that a slight jerk loosens it and puts it in his hands in one movement. This is more to be feared than his six-shooter, as his aim with it in absolutely unerring. I have seen him catch a steer, going at full speed, by any foot he desired. He can do this nine in ten times. And it is this, coupled with his horsemanship, which is part of the art of throwing the lariat (lasso), which makes the Texas cowboy so famous. He can ride anything in the way of a horse. He lassos a wild horse, claps a saddle on him, blinds him, and mounts, strips the blinds off, and then calmly sits on the pony's hurricane deck while he pitches all over the prairie trying to unseat the rider. As soon as the pony is bridle wise he is trained to help in the lasso throwing. This consists in teaching the horse to run after straying members of a herd until he sees the lasso shoot out in front of him, and feels a pull a slight pull-on the bridle, when he must suddenly stop, throw himself on his haunches, and brace his fore feet in front with all his might. This brings the steer to the ground, as the lasso is made fast to the horn of the saddle, and is as firm as if tied to a post when that little pony braces himself so. The cowboy sometimes throws this lasso over a tenderfoot, or even brings an enemy to bay with it. He also uses it as a means of amusing himself and companions in this way:

  He gets on his pony and has another well trained one ready and induces some city man, who thinks he is a rider from "way back" because he has attended an equestrian school, to mount. Then be gives the stranger a few lessons in lasso throwing, and they start out after a "beef" that is driven from the herd. The ponies give chase, and the tenderfoot manages finally to throw his lasso over the head of the flying steer. As soon as the trained pony sees the lasso fix itself over the head of the recalcitrant steer he knows it is time for him to do his part, and he does it, too quick as lightning he stops, throws his fore feet out in front, draws his hind feet under him, and his career of thirty miles an hour is suddenly reduced to a halt. Not so with his astonished rider, who keeps right on and shoots over the head of the astonished pony, who is amazed to see his rider flying twenty feet ahead of him plowing up a furrow in the hard, virgin prairie with his nose. The pony, too well trained to move until the steer either gets up and makes off again or is loosened, sits there with ears thrown forward and nostrils distented, trembling at the unusual sight. The only one who does not enjoy the spectacle, except his late rider. After this experience, which the cowboys call "initiating a tenderfoot," the Eastern man ceases to brag about his horsemanship and soon learns to be as expert as the best of the natives.

 The marksmanship of the Texas cowboy is a marvel also. He can gallop at full speed and hit a jack rabbit running with his pistol or Winchester. Some of them become so accurate in their aim while thus riding at full gallop that they can throw up a tin cup and put two and three bullets in it before it reaches the ground. It is their ability in this line which makes the Eastern writer give them the name of being desperadoes. The Texas cowboy has never been the desperado of the

Lone Star State. True, some of the cowboys have been bad men; but the rule is the opposite with the Texas cowboy. He hates the desperado, and has never been afraid of him, rather rejoicing in the opportunity offering to "down" the professional and swaggering bully and murderer. The Texas cowboy has never been afraid of anything or anybody. Hence his name. But he is full of good impulses, and will stand no nonsense. His greatest delight is in "downing" those who think to take him in, and he will fight if pushed into it, though usually waiting till he is compiled to do so or take "back water," as he calls it. This latter he never does.

And even that style of cowboy I have pictured, which is the genuine Texas cowboy, can no longer be found in Texas, except away out on the extreme border of the "territory" and along the Rio Grande. He has been crowded out by the wire fence, which makes it no longer necessary to herd cattle. The cowboy can flourish only where he has to "stand guard and herd" day in and day out, in all kinds of weather, sometimes being several days and nights in the saddle without sleeping, except napping in his seat on his pony. This he does frequently.

To see him in town is not to recognize him except by that peculiar walk noticeable to a close observer as belonging to a man who spends most of his time on horseback. It is a walk that resembles a cross between a man trying to step over potato hills and one trying to lift himself over a fence by his suspenders. He can be found mostly In Western and Northwestern Texas and in Wyoming Territory. In the cities he dresses in the best, is modest and quiet in manners, observes everything around him, puts up at the best hotels, and is lavish in spending his money. The few "drivers" who come to Chicago to bring cattle are not cowboys. They are simply drivers, and are held in supreme contempt by the real cowboy. The Texas cowboy of yesterday is the cattle king of today.

## THE DEMON STEER.
### A Horned Terror Even to the Dare-Devil Cowboys of the Plains.

The *Lyons Republican* **(Lyons, Kansas) 26 Sep 1889.** — George Wilson, a well-known cowboy, arrived from the northern ranges yesterday afternoon, says a Cheyenne, (Wyo.) letter to the Omaha Republican. According to Wilson there has roamed on the ranges adjacent to the Platte and Laramie rivers for these many years a mastodon wild steer whose aggressiveness and power make him the dread of every round up outfit. This combative beef bears not a brand, but no "rustler" dare appropriate him.

"The demon steer," as the pugnacious brute is called, knows no fear, and with lowered head, glistening eyes and sonorous bellow will charge upon anything in his course. Time upon time has he been rounded up with his comparative docile companions, but he invariably rushes past the line of riders as if no such obstruction to his flight existed. Once a CY outfit determined to effect the capture of the big fellow, but after he had gored two horses and scared the wits from half a dozen riders the undertaking was abandoned.

This prairie terror only last season in a fit of rage at those who dared intrude on the peaceful solitude of the range-charged at mid-day into a camp, creating a panic to which was ideal quietness the clatter incident to the stampede of the fabled bull in the imaginary china-shop. There was grand scattering of equipage and a disordered flight of the diners. One of these latter was so incensed that contrary to all orders he sent a six-shooter ball through the massive Steer, but the missile flow wide of its mark.

Wilson asserts that he will undertake to prove that the "demon steer" killed a big bear in a fair fight on the Sabylle three years ago and the cowboys will bet all their earthly belongings that Demon can conquer any bull in the territory. The combat with the bear was a terrible affair. Bruin was forced to the defensive from the start and for a time pluckily met the fearful onslaughts of the fighting steer, jarring the great form with blows from his paws. The activity of the steer was marvelous. He played around his antagonist as the sparrer annoys his foe and at nearly every charge ran his long, sharp horns into the blood-matted sides of the bear with the wicked "swish" of the effective sword-thrust. Wilson thinks the "demon steer will die of old age. The man who attempts his capture takes his life in his hands.

## FROZEN TO DEATH.

### Fearful Experience of a Party of New Mexico Cowboys.

**The *Evening Republican* (Meadville, Pennsylvania) 5 Nov 1889.** — Denver, Colo., Nov. — One of the results of the terrible blizzards which swept over eastern Colorado and northern New Mexico Thursday and Friday of last week, reached here today from Folsom, N. M. Thursday night Henry Miller, the range foreman for Col. Head, with several cowboys, camped near Sierra Grande with eighteen hundred cattle. At 4 o'clock that morning a blizzard from the northwest struck the herd, driving the cattle toward Panhandle, Tex. The snow was so blinding that it made it impossible to see fifty feet ahead.

Miller called his men together, and they started to follow the herd, and made an attempt to keep them bunched so far as possible. They became separated and Friday night one of them wandered into Head's home ranche, half dead with cold and hunger. He told his story, and a rescuing party was immediately sent out and at noon the frozen bodies of Henry Miller, Joe Martin and Charlie Jolly were found lying on the plains not far from Folsom. The other men succeeded in finding their way into camp before being overcome with cold.

# REMINGTON'S PICTURES.

## A Talk With the Artist, and Drawings From His Pen.

### How He Happened to Become an Artist. Peculiarities of the American Horse. Few Men Who Can Draw the Western Horse.

**The *Daily Times* (Davenport, Iowa) 19 Nov 1889.** — In a cozy little house in Mott Haven, New York City, just beyond the Harlem river, lives Frederic Remington, famous in the magazine world for his drawing of the horse. Readers of the great weeklies and monthlies find a fascination the life and nature of his work. He gained his position as an illustrator almost in a single bound. Four years ago he was a ranchman of the Southwest, without art training, making an occasional sketch or two for amusement in the interval of cowboy life.

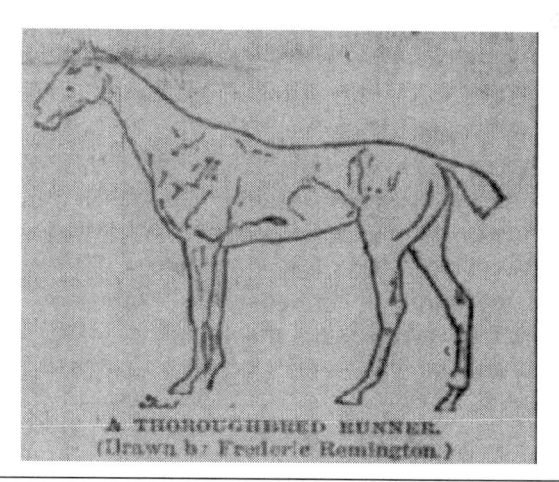

A THOROUGHBRED RUNNER.
(Drawn by Frederic Remington.)

In the spring of '86 he climbed up the stairs to the art editor of *"Harper's Weekly"* with a couple of sketches on the Indians and horses in the war of Geronimo, the Apache chief. He had just returned from that country at the end of his ranch life. A Yale College man, in 1879 he started out to make his fortune ranching in the far West. An expert horseman, a shrewd and keen observer from the start, he soon rose from a cowboy into a cattleman. The distinction on the plains is this: The owner of the ranch is the cattleman, the employee whatever his age may be, the cowboy. Thus, grizzled old frontiersmen are often the "boys," the wealthy youngster from the East the "man." But Remington's ranch did not prosper. The Indian troubles and hard luck pressed down upon him, and in '86 he gave it up as a failure and came on East. Here, "down on his luck," he determined to make a trial of his artistic propensities, fostered only by a bare month's study at the Yale Art School years before. His perfect understanding of the horse and his close observation during seven years of ranching now stood him in good stead.

In these trial sketches handed to *Harper's* there was a great lack of technique. They bore no comparison with the finished work of the regular staff. Yet there was in them a wide knowledge of the West, a reproduction of horse action, photographically wrong, but one that could be felt as correct. *Harpers'* not only accepted the sketches but sent him hack to Arizona for others.

His first sketches of Geronimo's campaign were printed late in the spring. Those he did on his special mission there appeared throughout the summer with a series of articles entitled, "Our Soldiers in the Southwest." During '87 and '88 appeared drawings of Mexican horses and men, frontier studies, Kansas cattle sketches and pictures of events in the East, such as racing and football scenes, and incidents on a man-of-war. But all this time it was as a drawer of the horse that he stood out most brightly. In the early part of 1888 he illustrated for the "Century" a series of papers written by Theodore Roosevelt on "Ranch Life in the Far West." Here he was in his element and his remembrance of his years in the saddle came forth in brilliantly graphic drawings of horse action. Later in the year he made drawings for Roosevelt's three "Century" articles, "Frontier Types." "Sheriff's Work on a Ranch," and "The Ranchman's Rifle on Crag and Prairie." His knowledge of technique was constantly increasing, and what he knew of horse anatomy was brought into still better. Within the last few months he illustrated for the "Century" written well four papers wonderings among the Indians and horses of the plains. Last winter, armed with letters from our War Department and accompanied by a detailed Mexican officer of engineers he visited the Mexican army in their camps and sketched the types. These sketches *"Harper's Magazine"* has just published. Besides these more important pieces of work, he has furnished countless sketches to various publications, and painted many characteristic scenes. But as a painter he makes no pretentions. He is purely an illustrator. Yet he works away conscientiously with his brush, looking toward the future in that.

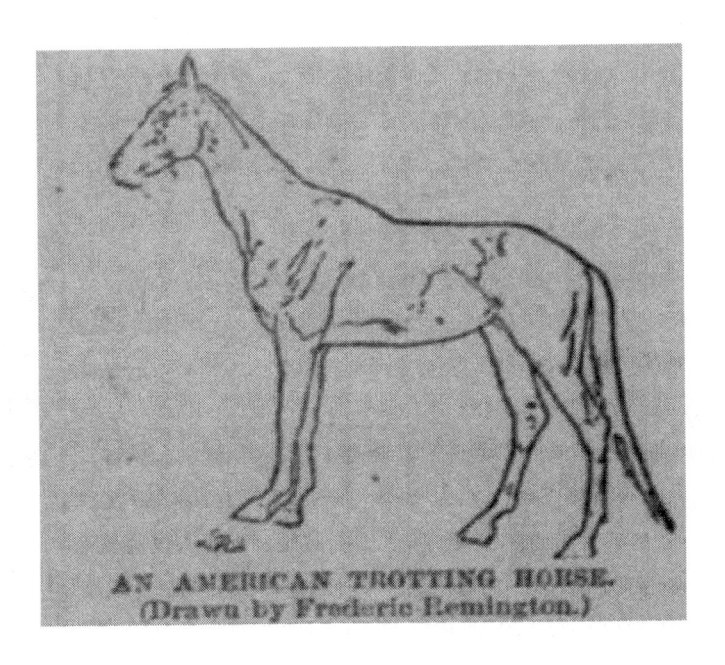

AN AMERICAN TROTTING HORSE.
(Drawn by Frederic Remington.)

Every year he spends several months In the West, picking up new material. When in New York, his afternoons are spent in the saddle, the mornings given up to work. His studio is a curious place. The walls are lined and the corners piled up with saddles and bridles and bits of trappings of the ranchman and the Mexican horseman. There are studies of all types of horses scattered about. Remington himself is a sturdy, stocky man of fine physique, tall, round faced and smooth shaven. He has the artistic temperament to a dot, but it is an athletic one. His ways of work and his ideas as are interesting as characteristic of the man who in three short years has attained a rank that most people work a life time for.

"It wasn't because I knew how to draw that I met with my success," he says, "for I didn't: but because I knew the West better than any other man. I have been all over it, from the City of Mexico to the Saskatchewan up North. They recognized a latent quality in my work which none other had.

"My drawing is done almost entirely from memory. I understand the horse so that every movement of his has fixed itself upon me. For a color effect, a hand or a fold in the sleeve, I sometimes use a model, but that is all. The model is inactive, there is a stiffness about it, and he struck an illustrative pose. "The subject is alive and in action. Nature doesn't pose."

As to drawing from a photograph, I am thoroughly familiar with all instantaneous photography, but I never, use the camera now, I haven't for a year past. The photograph lacks the interest which I seem to be able to give to horse action. And the best attestation of that is that my horse is incorrectly drawn from the photographic standpoint. We know that the photograph must be correct, but it doesn't give the impression. Now, it is very easy for the artist who knows how these horses move to observe and feel the motion, and then reproduce it.

People have no time to look at the common place. The interesting never occurs in nature as a whole, but in, pieces. It rarely ever happens that one gets a thoroughly good picture from a photograph.

It's more what I leave out than what I add. I merely fix the salient points.

I think this: If one desires to successfully draw the horse he should know the type and the differences, for horses are as different as men. What success I have had has been because I have a horseman's knowledge of a horse. No one can draw equestrian subjects unless he is an equestrian himself. The most of our American horse artists live in the middle of New York and aren't out among horses. These are the men, who, in a picture will put an Indian on a $700 horse instead of the scrubby pony he really rides. Knowing the type it is next the task to delineate it. Then the object is accomplished.

The matter of saddlery and frontier trappings, the perfect knowledge of them, opens up another and a very wide subject.

The Poles and the Russians, as a nation, are the best horse artists. They not only paint and draw them but they lead the world in their horse modeling in bronze. Chilmunsky and Kowalsky are the most famous of those modelers. In Poland and Russia there is a wide diversity of horse stock and strain, ranging from the thoroughbred in the cities to the Cossack pony. Those people live closer to their horses than we do here. There is a great deal in the liking of a horse to be able to draw him well. But the American artist should easily lead, it would seem, with such a variety of types as we have, the Western pony the American trotting horse, and the thoroughbred runner. Those only need to be strongly individualized to win success. Now there is too much sameness in the horses of England.

THE WESTERN PONY.
(Drawn by Frederic Remington.)

In France, though the artists paint magnificently, they hadn't the knowledge of the horse bar Rosa Bonheur and perhaps Moreau, who, they say, doesn't rely on models at all.

The outline sketches accompanying this were drawn by Mr. Remington to illustrate what he has here said. The individuality of the types is certainly very strongly marked.

**CROMWELL CHILDE.**

**THANKS FOR READING!
DON'T FORGET TO REVIEW ON AMAZON.
and
GOODREADS.**

# Glossary

agricultural, 38
Arizona, 29, 31, 34, 181, 209
Big Horn, 171
Boston, ix
buffalo, 39, 42
buffalo grass, 39, 42
Canon City, 41
cattle, 51, 52, 53, 104, 109, 125, 129, 130, 131, 134, 135, 136, 173
cattle men, 42, 45
cattlemen, 85
Cheyenne, 50, 51, 52, 53, 103, 105, 125, 205
Colorado, ii, 1, 3, 29, 36, 37, 38, 41, 55, 56, 60, 61, 64, 65, 80, 82, 83, 84, 86, 87, 88, 90, 92, 94, 104, 119, 147, 150, 207, 220
cowboy, 89, 90, 109, 110, 175, 205
CY, 205
Dakota, 53, 55, 56, 65, 80, 96, 97, 98, 99, 104, 125, 139, 140, 146, 160, 178
Denver, 36, 37, 39, 42, 155
Fetterman, 91
Garden of the Gods, 38
Glen Eyrie, 38
Johnson county, 53
Laramie, 51, 137, 205
lariat, 109
lasso, 108, 109
Manitou, 37

Montana, 1, 21, 23, 47, 55, 56, 65, 80, 101, 111, 112, 120, 143, 150, 183
Mormon, 130
Nebraska, 1, 17, 28, 41, 55, 59, 61, 66, 70, 104
Nevada, 1, 36, 55, 65
New Mexico, 5, 29, 34, 39, 41, 65, 72, 73, 157, 168, 207, 220
North Platte, 52, 104
Pike's Peak, 37
Powder River, 50
Pueblo, 36
railroad, 45, 50
ranch, 51, 102, 105
Rio Grande, 37
Rocky, 45, 173
San Juan, 40
sheep, 54
Southeast Colorado, 16
stampede, 133, 174, 206
Swan, 50, 51
Sweetwater, 137
tenderfeet, 89
tenderfoot, 172
Texas, 1, 5, 9, 10, 11, 23, 29, 30, 41, 45, 47, 49, 52, 53, 55, 56, 61, 62, 88, 92, 94, 104, 125, 140, 147, 149, 150, 164, 177, 181, 186, 188, 190, 197, 198, 200, 201, 203, 204
Utah, 1, 17, 55, 65
Ute Pass, 38

Washington, 55, 64, 65, 73
wild horses, 103, 104, 105, 172, 173, 174
Wyoming, ii, 1, 13, 16, 17, 21, 23, 26, 35, 41, 45, 52, 53, 55, 56, 60, 61, 64, 65, 99, 100, 104, 121, 128, 136, 143, 174, 204, 220

## About Kent

Kent Brooks is the author of *"Old Boston: As Wild As They Come,"* has worked in higher education managing Information Technology and Distance Learning departments for colleges in New Mexico, Oklahoma and Wyoming for more than 20 years.

Growing up in Springfield, Colorado he listened to southeast Colorado stories about broomcorn, the dust bowl and cowboys of the large cattle companies. He is a long time blogger on various technology topics for his own blog KentBrooks.com as well as the local history blog Bacacountyhistory.com which covers topics about Baca County, Colorado, the most southeast county in Colorado. He currently works for Casper College in Casper, Wyoming.

Made in the USA
Middletown, DE
24 November 2018